BION IN BUENOS AIRES

BION IN BUENOS AIRES
Seminars, Case Presentation, and Supervision

Edited by
Joseph Aguayo, Lia Pistiner de Cortinas, and Agnes Regeczkey

Routledge
Taylor & Francis Group
LONDON AND NEW YORK

First published 2018 by
Karnac Books Ltd.

Published 2018 by Routledge
2 Park Square, Milton Park, Abingdon, Oxon OX14 4RN
711 Third Avenue, New York, NY 10017, USA

Routledge is an imprint of the Taylor & Francis Group, an informa business

British Library Cataloguing in Publication Data

A C.I.P. for this book is available from the British Library

ISBN-13: 9781782205203 (pbk)

Typeset by Medlar Publishing Solutions Pvt Ltd, India

CONTENTS

PART IV: BION'S FURTHER SUPERVISORY WORK WITH OTHER ARGENTINIAN ANALYSTS

PART V: BION'S DIALOGUE WITH THE AUDIENCE ON QUESTIONS ABOUT SUPERVISION

ACKNOWLEDGEMENTS

The rescue of lost but valuable manuscripts that illuminate the history of our field is a communal endeavour. In this effort, it was occasioned by Agnes Regeczkey's Christmas holiday visit to Buenos Aires in December 2015, one that led to a meeting with Lia Pistiner de Cortinas. She had in hand a small surprise, namely the manuscript of Wilfred Bion's 1968 *Clinical Seminars in Buenos Aires*. Originally recorded in English, these *Clinical Seminars* were in turn faithfully translated into Spanish by Lia's colleague and dear friend, Elizabeth Tabak de Bianchedi. While these seminars had not been in wide circulation among Argentinian analysts, upon Agnes Regeczkey's return to Los Angeles, we immediately sought out help from Karnac Books in London. We owe Oliver Rathbone a debt of gratitude in so far as he saw the value of these recovered seminars, and through his intercession we procured the rights to publish them courtesy of Nicola Bion and the Marsh Agency. He was also instrumental in having the Spanish text capably translated in its entirety into English by Beatrice Sadovy. To my cousin, Dr Luis Arevalo, we also owe a profound debt for his generosity in re-reading and translating difficult passages of this Bion manuscript. I would also like to thank

Sira Dermen, Robert Hinshelwood, and the late Jim Grotstein for many years of spirited clinical and historical discussions about Bion's work.

I would also like to acknowledge the analyst/members of the private Bion study group that has been meeting in the United States for some years now. For some months prior to the publication of the *Bion in Buenos Aires Clinical Seminars*, this group discussed various seminars from the manuscript; and I have felt bolstered by our group in seeing these seminars into print by virtue of the spirited exchanges we have had in our meetings. So many thanks to: Caron Harrang, Dana Blue, Maxine Nelson (Seattle); Deborah Sandy, David Brooks, Agnes Regeczkey (Los Angeles); and finally, Susan Finkelstein and Marilyn Rifkin (New York City), and Marie Murphy (Washington, DC). Last and not least, to my wife Marina, who had the grace to tolerate her husband's late-night preoccupations with archival manuscripts.

Joseph Aguayo

I want to express my gratitude to Darío Sor, who was my analyst and by whom I was later supervised and with whom I studied Freud, Melanie Klein, and Bion. And also to Elizabeth T. de Bianchedi, by whom I was also supervised and studied Freud, Melanie Klein, and Bion, and who was also a very dear friend. Both Darío Sor and Elizabeth T. de Bianchedi were very generous people and stimulated my own development as a psychoanalyst and later on as an author of books related to Bion's ideas. With both of them, we organised the first Bion Conference in Buenos Aires in 1999, and these conferences became a tradition that now take place every two years in South America, North America, and Europe.

Lia Pistiner de Cortinas

I would like to express my gratitude to Hector, my husband, for his enormous support and encouragement to stay true to my heart and pursue my dreams; to my mother, father, and grandparents for endlessly loving me as a child; to Joseph Aguayo for his guidance and passion for the clinical history of our field; to Lia Pistiner de Cortinas for her sincere dedication throughout this project; Luis Arevalo for his wonderful contribution in the translation of the material; to my analytic family, teachers, colleagues, and candidates at the New Center for Psychoanalysis for the gift of psychoanalytic experience and education; to Allen Bishop and the faculty at Reiss Davis for their inspiration in my research; to my past, present, and future students and patients who have faith that dreams come true; to Donald Marcus for his contagious love and compassion while roaming the uncharted terrains of the unconscious.

Agnes Regeczkey

ABOUT THE EDITORS

Joseph Aguayo is a training and supervising analyst at the Psychoanalytic Center of California and is in private practice in West Los Angeles. He is also a guest member of the British Psychoanalytical Society in London. He holds doctorates in both clinical psychology and European history from the University of California, Los Angeles. He has been awarded a number of research fellowships from the International Psychoanalytical Association's Research Advisory Board, and has merged his clinical and research interests through numerous publications over the last twenty years in the *International Journal of Psychoanalysis* on the clinical history of Kleinian and Bionian psychoanalysis.

He conducts private teleconferences on many aspects of Wilfred Bion's work, for example, the psychosis papers and many of Bion's clinical seminars. He also serves as the main Chair for the Regional Bion Symposium, a yearly conference that gathers American analytic colleagues interested in furthering their understanding of Bion's work. Aguayo's last book was a co-edited project with Barnet Malin, *Bion's Los Angeles Seminars and Supervision* (Karnac, 2013). He has published a full-length book review of Wilfred Bion's sixteen-volume Complete Works for the *International Journal of Psychoanalysis* (Feb., 2017). His previous *International Journal of Psychoanalysis* publication was in 2014: "Bion's "Notes on memory and desire": its initial clinical reception in the United States—a note on archival material".

Lia Pistiner de Cortinas is a training analyst, full member of the Argentine Psychoanalytical Association (SAP), and fellow of the International Psychoanalytical Association (IPA). She has a specialisation in child and adolescent psychoanalysis. She is professor of postgraduate seminars at the Faculty of Psychology of the Buenos Aires University, and on Bion's ideas that transform clinical practice and on psychosomatic pathologies. These courses are taught at the University Institute of Mental Health of Buenos Aires Psychoanalytic Association.

Her publications include: her books *The Aesthetic Dimension of the Mind: Variations on a Theme of Bion* (Karnac, 2009) and *On Mental Growth: Bion's Ideas that Transform the Psychoanalytic Clinical Practice* (Buenos Aires: Ed. Biebel, 2011; to be published in English by Karnac); with E. T. de Bianchedi and others, the co-authored work *Bion conocido/desconocido* (Bion known/unknown); "Science and fiction in the psychoanalytical field", a chapter in *Bion Today* (London & New York: Routledge, 2011); *Autismo: una perspectiva psicoanalitica* (Buenos Aires: Ed. Biebel, 2015); contributor on Bion to *The Edinburgh International Encyclopedia of Psychoanalysis* (Edinburgh University Press, 2007); "Transcending the Caesura: the road towards insight", a paper in *Building on Bion: Branches* (London: Jessica Kingsley, 2003).

Agnes Regeczkey is a candidate at the New Center for Psychoanalysis. She holds a doctorate in psychology and works in private practice in Palos Verdes, California. With an interest in interdisciplinary aspects of psychoanalytic theories, Regeczkey teaches research and dissertation development and is a research coordinator at Reiss-Davis Graduate Center, Los Angeles. Her academic research includes: psychoanalytic history, interfacing perspectives of neuroscience and psychoanalytic theories, and how psychoanalysis may be used as a preventative treatment modality for young children and their families.

Regeczkey has been an active participant in various Bionian study groups, such as a nationwide conference group studying Bion's Italian and Brazilian clinical seminars, and the yearly Regional Bion Symposium held in Los Angeles. Regeczkey presented a paper in Budapest at the Hungarian Psychoanalytic Society, 9 and 10 October 2015, titled "Love, hate, and identity at the inception of psychoanalytic theories—inseparable reality of theory and theorists". In co-authorship with J. Aguayo, they published "Small group collaborators and adversaries in the London Kleinian development", *Psychoanalytic Quarterly* (July 2016). In 2016 and 2017, with the collaboration of the New Center for Psychoanalysis, she organised and led two André Haynal seminars, exploring the intricate historical confluence of Freud, Jung, and Ferenczi, and political movements involved in the early history of psychoanalysis.

FOREWORD

Little has been discussed about Bion's approach to clinical work. His terse published paper on memory and desire (Bion, 1967) was too short to give a rounded picture, and merely created perplexed and confused readers; the long treatise in the latter part of his book *Second Thoughts* seems to have been rarely considered. So, it appears that when Bion was fêted around the world and gave lectures on three continents, he did relent from his beloved abstractions and entered the far from abstract work of listening to patients. This book is a godsend in giving us some insight into Bion's approach by examining in detail a series of hitherto unknown seminars. The editors are to be congratulated on having retrieved the record from the mists of historical time, and second, for taking us through Bion's words so carefully. They have retrieved a clinical Bion only slowly emerging so long after his lifetime.

Unlike his theoretical thinking, which is interrupted by a number of caesuras (Torres & Hinshelwood, 2013), his clinical approach has a consistency. It is *always* about making sense of a subjective experience. As he wrote in 1948, in his group period: "I do not feel quite as happy about postulating a transference as I do about postulating a countertransference" (Bion, 1948, p. 65). From this period, Bion worked very much with his countertransference, his own experience. He was at the time, during his psychoanalytic training, in supervision with Paula Heimann, the author of the landmark paper on countertransference (1950), which she wrote in 1949, almost contemporary with Bion's comment just given. Bion carries this sensitivity to his own reactions through all the rest of his clinical life, it seems.

The crucial book in this respect was Bion's *Attention and Interpretation* published in 1970 (only two years after the Buenos Aires visit) but drawing from published and unpublished papers going back to the mid-1960s. In that book, he was trying to conceptualise how to attend to and understand (or interpret) the analyst's experience. He used different abstract terms (and designed his nearly incomprehensible "Grid"). But in general shape his idea of the proto-mental life in groups (Bion, 1950) had transformed into the "evolution" of an idea in the analyst's mind, that is, the selected fact (Bion, 1967), and eventually the intuitions about the patient's suffering as he described it in 1970. These published words of his that I list are all very well, but it is outstanding to have this living record of Bion's attempt to put flesh on these skeleton abstractions.

At this point, 1968, Bion seems to be working out the use of intuition in this more spontaneous phase of his work. It comes to fruition in 1970 when he attempted to capture the difference between feeling and suffering. In 1970: "We find it necessary to differentiate between the pain of a broken leg and the pain, say, of bereavement" (Bion, 1970, p. 6). It is that difference of attention that, it seems to me, Bion was always clutching at. We sort of "know", from inside as it were, what the heartache is. The psychoanalyst knows what a bereavement is like, not from touch, sight, smell, and so on. It is different from knowing a leg is broken, a pain that has to be alleviated with anaesthetics or analgesics. The intuited suffering of a broken heart is something that needs… well, to be suffered. Psychoanalysts should not make do with perceiving the visible signs of a patient's symptoms, the structure of his personality, the dynamics of the instinctual energy, in the way a doctor in casualty will assess a fractured leg—the swelling, deformity, the groans of the patient, and so on. If we pay attention to that level of evidence, we avoid the true nature of psychoanalytic evidence.

Bion was almost obsessive in presenting this distinction, which characterised his group work period (1943–1952) and then again from the mid-1960s. In the 1950s, he did present clinical work, but it was different. He fell into the trap, I think, of a more mechanical scientific thinking based on theory. And not surprisingly, he went back on most of it (Bion, 1967).

In his published work, he made his plea for intuition in conceptual terms. It is a strong message, and one Bion tried to draw out from his wide reading of Keats, Kant, and the Christian mystics. But, from around 1967, he conducted many clinical seminars around the world on three continents. And in this clinical focus he comes out in a new guise, no longer abstract and literary, he presented his clinical work in Buenos Aires (in Seminar Five); and commented in reflective detail on the clinical work of others, notably Horatio Etchegoyen's case, in Seminars Six and Seven. Here, he surveyed the psychoanalytic terrain in his allusive and intuitive way in the Seminars themselves. He introduces the method by demonstrating that capacity for spontaneous evolution in front of his audience, in real time.

Is this something new, or is it just a throwback to days when we were not constrained by the rigours of Enlightenment materialism? The medieval mystics could feel in touch with the infinite, although Bion now knows it as the Unconscious.

Later, his method of giving his audience an experience of his associative intuition was more extreme. As Francesca, his wife, commented: "for those looking for cut-and-dried 'answers' Bion's method was inexplicable, frustrating and aggravating ... He believed that 'La reponse est le malheur de la question'" (Bion, 1970, p. vii). And of the Brazilian Lectures, I once wrote: "he does not intend that his audiences should find it easy; nor that they should ever be allowed to think that they understand. These lectures are a constant challenge to the knowingness of his audience" (Hinshelwood, 1992, p. 124). But by then, he was back to abstraction. Perhaps he thought that presented clinical material could so easily be distorted by his audiences into preconceived knowledge. We must make the most of the window into the clinic that Joe Aguayo and his colleagues have given us here.

The question Bion poses to you, Reader, is whether you can get out of that positivist line of medical thinking, to gauge a modality of thought that Bion believed to be both ancient and yet still to be achieved?

R. D. Hinshelwood

References

Bion, W. R. (1948). Group methods of treatment. In: *The Complete Works of W. R. Bion, Volume 4* (pp. 65–70). London: Karnac, 2014.

Bion, W. R. (1950). Experiences in groups, VI. In: *Human Relations, Volume 3* (pp. 395–402). [Republished in W. R. Bion, *Experiences in Groups and Other Papers* (pp. 115–126). London: Tavistock Publications, 1961; and in *The Complete Works of W. R. Bion, Volume 4* (pp. 186–195). London: Karnac, 2014.]

Bion, W. R. (1967). *Second Thoughts*. London: Heinemann. [Republished in *The Complete Works of W. R. Bion, Volume 6* (pp. 53–202). London: Karnac, 2014.]

Bion, W. R. (1970). *Attention and Interpretation*. London: Tavistock. [Republished in *The Complete Works of W. R. Bion, Volume 6* (pp. 219–330). London: Karnac, 2014.]

Hinshelwood, R. D. (1992). Brazilian Lectures: 1973, Sao Paulo; 1974, Rio de Janeiro/Sao Paulo. *International Review of Psycho-Analysis, 19*: 123–126.

Torres, N., & Hinshelwood, R. D. (2013). *Bion's Sources: The Shaping of His Paradigms*. London: Routledge.

INTRODUCTION

Bion in the New World—from Los Angeles to Buenos Aires

Joseph Aguayo

This brief introduction opens with two short pieces, the first of which begins with Bion in Los Angeles in 1967. He would henceforth continue a decade-long odyssey of clinical seminars in all three regions of the International Psychoanalytic Association. Bion's *Los Angeles Clinical Seminars* (2013) in turn set the context for his work in Buenos Aires, and there, some of their analysts, such as León Grinberg, had some familiarity with Bion's ideas when he arrived there in late July 1968.

By the time Wilfred Bion had lived and worked in Los Angeles for a few months in 1968, he re-routed himself from a family holiday in England, stopped off at the recently rededicated John F. Kennedy Airport in New York to change planes quickly, and then made his way to Buenos Aires. There, he was to teach and supervise for the next two weeks in late July/early August (Bion, *CW* 2, pp. 172–173). He was greeted by León Grinberg, who, having heard Bion at International Psychoanalytic Association Congresses, had already formed a small study group of

Argentinian analysts interested in furthering their understanding of his ideas. The larger number of South American analysts who came to hear Bion in 1968 arrived with some familiarity with Kleinian ideas, while fewer directly knew Bion's published work (Grinberg, in Talamo-Bion, Borgogno, & Merciai, 2000, p. xx).

This situation in Buenos Aires was somewhat dissimilar from the experience Bion had had in April 1967 at the Los Angeles Psychoanalytic Society and Institute, where he had come to teach and supervise—before he decided to live and work there. The visitor now became a resident of Los Angeles. Making the assumption that American-trained ego analysts would not be very familiar with his ideas about the Kleinian understanding and treatment of near psychotic and psychotic cases, Bion emphasised this aspect as he also informed American analysts about the latest Kleinian ideas on technique, namely working in the "here and now". On the other hand, since Melanie Klein's ideas had been in vogue for some time after the Second World War in Argentina, there was more familiarity with her work, more with child than psychotic patients (Etchegoyen & Zysman, 2005).

On the American front, Bion's recent ideas about technique were also the source of bewilderment and criticism among American analysts, especially those who were asked to comment on his brief sketch, "Notes on memory and desire" (Bion, 1967, pp. 272–280; 2013, pp. 133–149). In urging these American analysts to "abandon memory and desire", I have maintained that Bion startled many of his listeners in Los Angeles, who were long accustomed to the rigours of the classical definition of the transference as a displacement from past to present. Such an understanding fit in quite well with the idea of slow and gradual reconstruction of infantile neurotic conflicts and traumas. However well that might have worked in the treatment of analysable neurotics in the United States, Bion maintained that severely disturbed patients required a different kind of understanding and technical approach (Aguayo, 2014).

In also expanding the Kleinian paradigm to include the subjective processing capacities of the analyst, now becoming more popularly known as "container/contained", Bion also introduced notions about how the subtle complexity of the analyst's own subjective processes had to be factored into the treatment of disturbed and disturbing patients. While these factors of the analyst's own subjective impact on his or her analytic work had been discussed and debated at the British

Psychoanalytical Society since the post-Second World War era in such papers as D. W. Winnicott's "Hate in the countertransference" (1949), Paula Heimann's "Countertransference" (1950), and Bion's revised version of "Group dynamics" (1955), these ideas were still new in the United States, where the ego psychological ideas of analysts like Annie Reich (1960) still held sway. In this view of countertransference, overly subjective reactions on the analyst's part were more likely to be seen as revealing gaps or inadequately analysed *lacunae* in the analyst—and thus required either further supervision or remedial analysis. In the British Kleinian view of Reich's work on countertransference, they would have regarded her definition as too restrictive, something that left out the impact on the analyst of the psychotic patient's jumbled and disorganising communications.

When Bion came to the Americas and relayed these newer views on the analyst's subjectivity—after all, the analyst now had to consider how he or she oscillated to and fro from the chaotic realm of the "paranoid/schizoid" to the "depressive" position, there was a clash of analytic cultures. It appeared that British Kleinians like Bion understood Freud's structural theory in a different way from American-trained ego-psychological analysts. This point was humorously brought home when one Los Angeles analyst asked Bion if he ever made "structural considerations". Bion replied that he considered "container/contained" such a structural consideration! (Bion, 2013, p. 92). This mix of analytic cultures made for a Kleinian/Freudian slight confusion of tongues, but it seemed that Bion ultimately found his reception in Los Angeles to his liking because a few short months later, at the age of seventy, he left the British Psychoanalytical Society and moved himself and his wife Francesca to Los Angeles. Lionised though he was in London, as both the President of the British Society from 1962 through 1965, and thereafter Chair of the Melanie Klein Trust, he resigned these posts to live the last decade of his life in Los Angeles.

By moving to America, Bion managed to become an important conveyor of the Kleinian diaspora, bringing his version of Kleinian ideas to analysts little familiar with Melanie Klein's 1946 project to conceptualise and psychoanalytically treat near psychotic and psychotic states of mind. Since the great majority of American-trained analysts at that time were medical psychiatrists, most of them had psychiatric patients whose treatment did not fit into an American ego psychology paradigm most suited for the walking well. So, for the most part, Los Angeles psychiatrists gave

Bion an attentive hearing when he spoke on the subject of psychosis. The Freudian group in Los Angeles had also maintained a bit of a maverick identity in so far as it was the only American institute that had welcomed Kleinian analysts like Hanna Segal, Herbert Rosenfeld, and now Wilfred Bion as regular visitors since the early 1960s (Kirsner, 2000).

The initially receptive atmosphere turned against their work within a few short years after Bion decided to now stay as a permanent resident in Los Angeles. In short, while welcomed as a visitor, his ongoing presence for all but a few was regarded with suspicion and weariness. By the 1970s, the chasm between the American Freudians such as Ralph Greenson and the few British Kleinians in Los Angeles became known as the "Time of Troubles" (Kirsner, 2000).

But that is another story. Let me end this part of my introduction by pointing out some of the textual continuities and discontinuities between the Los Angeles and Buenos Aires Seminars. To start with the obvious: after years of writing dense and opaque epistemological monographs, Bion (1962, 1963, 1965) decided to distil his clinical thinking in the form of clinical supervisions and case presentations. Very few in attendance at the Los Angeles and Buenos Aires Seminars would have realised that Bion had been long disinclined to discuss extensive clinical case material in his writings, especially during the 1960s. There was scarcely any clinical material to be found in three theory-laden monographs, so it would been hard except for a few close colleagues in London to have much of an idea of how exactly Bion analysed his patients (Bion, 1962, 1963, 1965).

But in the Los Angeles Seminars, Bion reversed himself by spending most of the Third and Fourth Seminars giving detailed clinical accounts of his distillation of the Kleinian method. This outstanding organising feature of the Los Angeles Seminars, along with a long supervision of an analytic case presented to him (Bion, 2013, pp. 107–131), certainly demonstrated Bion's readiness to convey how he worked with especially disturbed patients to a group of soon-to-be colleagues on whom he would also depend for referrals once he relocated to Los Angeles just a few months later.[1]

This emphasis on the presentation and supervision of clinical material now became a signature of the clinical seminars for the next decade.[2]

Of particular interest here is Bion's presentation in his Third Los Angeles Seminar of a borderline case of a screaming, quite reproachful patient who made such an emotional cacophony of his consulting room that he concluded in exasperation, "I couldn't even hear myself think". It seems that a case can be made that this patient was so difficult to treat that Bion made a decision to keep presenting material from this case the next year in Buenos Aires (cf. Bion's Fifth Seminar). It is either that or there is simply an uncanny resemblance between these two patients. In electing for the former view, I think that this case in effect forms one of the longest case presentations by Bion we have gathered thus far, one that helps us understand something of what, in effect, was his implicit method of clinical inquiry. We also see how vulnerable a presenter Bion could be, in so far as he was exasperated to the point that he himself broached the issue with the patient of terminating the analysis. We are appreciative of having this long clinical example which gives us an opportunity to understand the various elements of his unique clinical approach, one whose careful study repays the analyst ten-fold in analysing his own difficult-to-treat patients.

Notes

1. Those familiar with Bion's early days in Los Angeles recall some initially worrisome months when very few came along to consult Bion (James Grotstein—personal communication).
2. One brief example from the Los Angeles Seminars that is relevant to clinical material presented in the Buenos Aires Seminars: in response to a query regarding overly agreeable patients, Bion briefly discussed a kind of patient who seemed to be in constant agreement with the analyst, but in "…terms which were extremely ambiguous". One particular patient exercised a masterly use of English and managed to get across a number of ambiguous meanings (Bion, 2013, p. 17). In the Buenos Aires Seminars, Bion discussed the countertransference problem of feeling annoyed with a patient who chronically agreed with his interpretations.

An introduction to Bion's Seminars in Buenos Aires

Lia Pistiner de Cortinas

In July/August 1968, Bion was invited by the Argentinian Psychoanalytic Association (APA) to lecture, give seminars and supervisions in Buenos Aires. Since the 1960s, and even long before, in Buenos Aires there was a great interest and enthusiasm for psychoanalysis, most of all Kleinian psychoanalysis. This interest resulted in many analysts studying and learning Kleinian ideas, but also in the fact that some Argentinian psychoanalysts went to London to be supervised by Melanie Klein. Dr Horacio Etchegoyen, who presented clinical material for the supervision with Bion, lived for some time in London and had his analysis with Donald Meltzer there in 1966.

The APA was created in 1942 and some of its members, such as Heinrich Racker, Marie Langer, and Angel Garma, came from Europe, taking refuge in Argentina because of Nazism or the Civil War in Spain. We can understand why these psychoanalysts left Europe, and we must keep in mind that the condition for developing a psychoanalytic movement is the existence of a state that respects the law and guarantees the freedom to teach psychoanalysis. This kind of state has a power over its citizens limited by the law, and without freedom it is not possible or it is very difficult to work as a psychoanalyst or teach psychoanalysis in specific institutions. To challenge all kinds of authoritarian manifestations is a contribution of psychoanalysis to society. The Faculty of Psychology was created in Buenos Aires in 1958, a few years after the government of Perón was overthrown by what seemed to be a liberal movement, called "La Revolución Libertadora"—and soon it had as professors well-known psychoanalysts, such as José Bleger, David Liberman, Rafael Paz, who in several books approached psychoanalytic subjects with very original hypotheses.

Unfortunately, I could not participate in the seminars and supervisions that Bion gave in Buenos Aires, because in the 1960s psychologists could not have access to the Argentinian Psychoanalytic Association, which was the only International Psychoanalytical Association in Argentina and which had invited Bion to come to Buenos Aires. The Military Government of the dictator General Onganía forbade psychologists to work as psychoanalysts. On the other hand, there were private study groups where psychoanalysts taught Freud, Melanie Klein, and

Bion. I was in one of these groups where we studied Bion with Elizabeth Tabak de Bianchedi, and also I was analysed by Darío Sor, supervised by Elizabeth Bianchedi, and later on, I was also supervised by Darío Sor. In those study groups and supervisions, I learned how Bion's ideas transformed our clinical practice.

In 1999, along with Elizabeth Bianchedi, Darío Sor, and other colleagues, I organised the Second International Bion Conference, which was held in Buenos Aires. James Grotstein and Gerard Bléandonu were the main speakers. The First International Bion Conference had been organised by Parthenope Bion-Talamo in Turin, two years earlier. In 1973, León Grinberg, Elizabeth Bianchedi, and Darío Sor wrote *Introducción a las Ideas de Bion* (*Introduction to the Work of Bion*), the first such book that gave an overview of his ideas and for which Bion himself wrote the foreword (Grinberg et al., 1973, 1975). Bion used as a model the emotional experience of seeing Vermeer's picture *The Little House in Delft*, comparing it with the impact of the emotional experience of reading this book.

With Elizabeth Bianchedi, Darío Sor, and a group of colleagues, we co-authored another book, *Bion/conocido-desconcido* (Bion, known/unknown), which was presented at the Bion Conference in Buenos Aires in 1999. That is how I began my work with Bion's ideas, his hypotheses about psychoanalytic theory and clinfical practice that later on resulted in my two books: *The Aesthetic Dimension of the Mind: Variations on a Theme of Bion* (Pistiner, 2009) and *Autismo: una perspectiva psicoanalitica* (Pistiner, 2016).

Buenos Aires, 1968: the psychoanalytic atmosphere

The professors of the Faculty of Psychology were almost all well-known psychoanalysts and psychologists, and several of them also worked in many of the hospitals of Buenos Aires. In the seminars and supervisions that Bion gave in Buenos Aires we can see an enthusiastic atmosphere towards psychoanalysis. Through the questions posed by many analysts, and Bion's spirited response, we realise the impact that his ideas had in Buenos Aires. The most significant subjects that Bion introduced in these seminars are placing psychoanalytic theory and clinical practice in a new dimension, one that nevertheless retained and refined most of the values of Freud's and Klein's contributions, while dealing with them from another perspective. Bion's originality stimulated a new attitude in the analyst.

Once again, Bion spoke about putting aside rigid schemas and clichés, and said that our work takes us down a lonely road. Psychoanalysts are alone in their work; their only companion is the patient, who is not reliable because of his defences. The depth of Bion's hypotheses, the flexibility of his models, and his recommendation to the analysts to work "*without memory, desire, and understanding*" attracted great attention in Buenos Aires, along with some uneasiness, which is reflected in the kinds of questions he received. In his published work, Bion's intention was to stimulate the creative capacity of the analyst, as if to say: "dare to think by yourself". At the same time, his interventions pointed towards the use of common sense, the development of psychoanalytic intuition, and an open state of mind towards "discovering".

Bion spoke about the difficulties of expressing new ideas with familiar, known words and explained that this led him to introduce terms without meaning, or to use known terms but with a very precise meaning. He insisted that in our work as psychoanalysts, we have to leave the meaning open-ended, so it can continue to evolve.

Approaching these seminars, one becomes aware not only of the emotional experience of reading them but also of the emotional experience for the analysts who were there in Buenos Aires, listening to Bion and asking him questions. For example, just to show some part of this vivid dialogue between Bion and his public: someone asked about external reality and Bion says that analysts meet a very peculiar reality in their work, and that this reality is almost impossible to communicate to anybody but the patient. The lateral communication, where one attempts to communicate what happens in analysis to one's colleagues, is not good. One can communicate this shared reality to the patient in the session, but the communication to the colleagues can be very difficult, if not impossible, because the experience of the analyst with his patient cannot be repeated with those who were not present in the session; it is a unique emotional experience.

Bion also spoke about the difficulties analysts have to face when their training is over; he stressed the difference between *speaking about analysis and analysing patients*. He referred to what cannot be learned through theory, and he spoke not only of psychoanalytic training but of the personal experience of the analyst developing his own technique. This implies knowing very few theories that have to become part of one's equipment. Memories and desire interfere between the analyst and reality: they interfere between the emotional experience that is taking place in the session with the patient: while the analyst is trying to resort to "what did the patient say yesterday?" or thinking "what will I do this weekend?", he is not present in the session. Analysts need to avoid bad habits, and Bion stressed that *his perspective on psychoanalysis implied throwing a penetrating dark beam that illuminated a dark zone.* He spoke of the need to develop a mental state of "patience" while not understanding and of "security" when the selected fact comes up and gives coherence to what was dispersed before.

In *Transformations* (1965), Bion uses a model for this aspect of his theory: the model is the reflection of a tree in a lake: the reflection will depend on the state of the lake, whether it is calm or stormy. In these seminars and in the dialogue with the analysts in Buenos Aires, one senses an analytic atmosphere of much interest; and in Bion, someone very favourably disposed towards dialogue. In these seminars, as it is with other works of Bion, one can perceive the strength and penetrating force of his ideas, ideas that contain doubts, mysteries, and uncertainties. To this kind of atmosphere we trust that the readers of this book will be exposed. The language Bion uses in these clinical seminars is easier to understand than his dense epistemological books simply because of the dialogue with the public.

A very interesting fact is that the analyst who presented the clinical material for extensive supervision with Bion was Dr Horacio Etchegoyen, who later on became the first Latin-American President of the International Psychoanalytic Association. While the original seminars were of course given by Bion in English, they were subsequently translated into Spanish by Elizabeth Bianchedi—and the editors had the task of securing help in retranslating this text back into English, a task that was ably handled by both Beatrice Sadovy and Dr Luis Arevalo.

Some of Bion's comments on the clinical material are very interesting: he says that that the psychoanalytic training is like a game, as serious and as amusing as a game. Analysts know about the problems that come up with patients who have inhibitions for playing and know that this inhibition is a very serious symptom. The child who cannot play is always a very disturbed patient. But analysts can repeat this error—of not playing—in a psychoanalytic treatment. Our psychoanalytic training is neither serious nor fun, and Bion says that it should be both: serious and fun. He remembers his psychoanalytic training as an experience that took place in a small and hot room, full of smoke, with an analyst who was exhausted, the same as the students—because besides the training they had to work a lot. Bion comments that it was nobody's fault, because analysis had to be taught and learned in the evenings that they had free, so he remembers his psychoanalytic training as one of the most terrible periods of his life, something we can also appreciate because, during much of his training, he had to (as a single parent) be away from his very young daughter, Parthenope.

It is also interesting the impact that Bion's visit to Buenos Aires had on the analysts who attended his seminars and supervisions, such as Jorge M. Mom, who was the president of APA, and Luisa Alvarez de Toledo, Madeleine and Willy Baranger, José Bleger, Elizabeth Tabak de Bianchedi, Diego García Reinoso, León and Rebeca Grinberg, David Liberman, Darío Sor (just to mention a few). This interest was also shown in the fact that, after his visit, the APA organised a scientific meeting where his seminars and supervisions, which had been recorded and distributed among the analysts, were discussed in small groups of analysts the whole day long, and these discussions were published by the APA, in a book that, as far as I know, remained in private circulation as an internal publication. Reading these discussions, we can see that these analysts were approaching different themes, such as the impact that Bion's personality had on them, his theoretical contributions, and the psychoanalytic clinical implications of his ideas. Some of the items approached in these discussions reflected the perceived distance between the "clinical" Bion and the "theoretical" Bion. The comments in the meeting—where these analysts were working through the emotional experience of his visit—were that the "screen" of opacity that seemed to separate each aspect disappeared when they could meet Bion and then understand the coherence of his ideas.

I close here by recounting one of my last visits with Dr Horacio Etchegoyen, just months before his lamentable death on 2 July 2016. When I asked him what he remembered of the clinical material he presented in these Buenos Aires Seminars, he simply said: "I don't really remember the patient, but having been supervised by Bion was a very interesting and extraordinary experience."

References

Aguayo, J. (2014). Bion's "Notes on memory and desire"—its initial clinical reception in the United States: a note on archival material. *International Journal of Psychoanalysis*, 95: 889–910.

Baranger, W. (1971). *Posición y Objeto en la Obra de Melanie Klein*. Buenos Aires: Ediciones Kargieman.

Bianchedi, E., Antar, R., Bianchedi, M., Cortinas, L., Dimant, S., Kaplan, A., Sáenz, M., & Oelsner, R. (1999). *Bion conocido/desconocido* (Bion known/ unkown). Buenos Aires: Editorial Lugar.

Bion, W. R. (1948). Group methods of treatment, in: *The Complete Works of W. R. Bion*, Vol. IV. London: Karnac.

Bion, W. R. (1955). On group dynamics: a review. In: M. Klein et al. (Eds.), *New Developments in Psychoanalysis* (pp. 22–239). London: Tavistock.

Bion, W. R. (1962). *Learning from Experience*. London: Heinemann [reprinted in paperback, London: Maresfield Reprints, H. Karnac Books, 1984].

Bion, W. R. (1963). *Elements of Psycho-Analysis*. London: William Heinemann Medical Books.

Bion, W. R. (1965). *Transformations*. London: William Heinemann Medical Books.

Bion, W. R. (1967a). Notes on memory and desire. *The Psychoanalytic Forum*, 2: 272–273; 279–290.

Bion, W. R. (1967b). *Second Thoughts*. New York: Basic Books.

Bion, W. R. (1970). *Attention and Interpretation*. London: Heinemann.

Bion, W. R. (1980). *Bion in New York and Sao Paolo*. Perthshire: Clunie Press.

Bion, W. R. (2013). *Wilfred Bion: Los Angeles Seminars and Supervision*. Ed. J. Aguayo & B. Malin. London: Karnac.

Bion, W. R. (2014). *The Complete Works of W. R. Bion*. Ed. C. Mawson, 16 volumes. London: Karnac.

Bleger, J. (1967). *Simbiosis y Ambigüedad*. Buenos Aires: Paidós.

Etchegoyen, H., & Zysman, S. (2005). Melanie Klein in Argentina: beginnings and development. *International Journal of Psychoanalysis*, 86: 869–894.

Grinberg, L. (2000). Foreword. In: *W. R. Bion—Between Past and Future*. Edited P. Bion-Talamo, F. Borgogno, & S. Merciai. London: Karnac.

Grinberg, L., Sor, D., & Tabak de Bianchedi, E. (1973). *Introducción a las Ideas de Bion*. Buenos Aires: Nueva Visión.

Grinberg, L., Sor, D., & Tabak de Bianchedi, E. (1975). *Introduction to the Work of Bion*. London: Roland Harris Trust.

Heimann, P. (1950). On countertransference. *International Journal of Psychoanalysis*, 31: 81–84.

Hinshelwood, R. D. (1983). Projective identification and Marx's concept of man. *International Review of Psychoanalysis*, 10: 221–226.

Kirsner, D. (2000). *Unfree Associations: Inside Psychoanalytic Institutes*. London: Process Press.

Klein, M. (1946). Notes on some schizoid mechanisms. *International Journal of Psychoanalysis*, 27: 99–110.

Liberman, D. (1971). *Lingüística comunicativa y proceso psicoanalítico*. Buenos Aires: Galerna.

Liberman, D., Grassano de Picolo, E., Neborak de Dimant, S., Pistiner de Cortiñas, L., & Roitman de Woskoboinik, P. (1982). *Del Cuerpo al Símbolo, sobreadaptación y enfermedad psicosomática*. Buenos Aires: Ediciones Kargieman.

Pistiner de Cortinas, L. (2007). *The Aesthetic Dimension of the Mind*. London: Karnac.

Pistiner de Cortinas, L. (2016). *Autismo, una perspectiva psicoanalítica*. Buenos Aires: Editorial Beibel.

Rodrigué, E., & de Rodrigué, T. G. (1966). *El Contexto del Proceso Psicoanalítico*. Buenos Aires: Paidós.

Sor, D., & Senet de Gazzano, M. R. (1988). *Cambio Catastrófico*. Buenos Aires: Ediciones Kargieman.

Torres, N., & Hinshelwood, R. D. (Eds.) (2013). *Bion's Sources: The Shaping of His Paradigms*. London: Routledge.

Winnicott, D. W. (1949). Hate in the countertransference. *International Journal of Psychoanalysis*, 30: 69–74.

PART I

BION'S CLINICAL SEMINARS

FIRST SEMINAR

A case vignette—countertransference—the analyst's subjectivity as a factor in clinical technique—abandonment of memory and desire—audience questions*

Mr President, ladies and gentlemen, I am quite grateful for your warm welcome and profoundly appreciate the opportunity to be here and to learn about the kind of work you are doing. I will try to explain something about my own experience.

On a certain occasion, I had a patient who was about thirty-one years old and who was rather cordial and cooperative. I refer now to what, in my opinion, could be described as quite a typical session at an early stage of any analysis. This kind of session was representative of the first year, though a certain annoyance I experienced stretched into the second year of the treatment.

The patient said that he had had a dream that he could not remember in detail. However, he did remember he had gone for a walk with his girlfriend, who had pointed at an object in the sky, while commenting that it was really noticeable. To her amazement, however, the patient could not see it. The patient believed that this was the entire dream. He went on to say he did not really consider her his girlfriend, but that he had known her for many years and that their friendship had acquired a

---

*This conference was presented at the Argentine Psychoanalytic Association on 30 July 1968.

more profound meaning in recent months. I interpreted that he felt me as a girlfriend or a sister, something he had never had, and that meant that having a relationship with some kind of analytic sister instead of a direct relationship with me had become important to him.

The patient was in complete agreement with me. At this stage of the treatment, I had started to experience something about the way in which I was conducting the analysis. I believed that up to that point I had not had enough material so as to make that interpretation. I was about to remind him of certain previous material which I had used as a basis of my formulation; in other words, I wanted to point out the kind of information I had. In a few words, I would have liked to have said: "Well, why do you think that is correct?" But it is hard to ask that question when the other person has just said, in their own opinion, that your interpretation is correct. The patient continued speaking and he said—somehow confirming my interpretation—that, in truth, his mother had told him of a sister of his who had died before his birth. He continued adding material that corroborated how appropriate my interpretation was. He concluded by stating that his mother would love to come to see me in order to talk to me about this question.

I replied by wondering why he thought his mother could tell me more about what I wanted to know than he could. I went on to say that there probably existed some reason why, at this stage of the analysis, he considered that his information was incomplete and that his mother would be able to provide me with more exact information about what was happening in his mind. The patient completely agreed with me; he admitted to being mistaken and added that it would be best if he himself gave me that information, which he did. He said that those objects had been described by his girlfriend as clouds of definite shapes, almost too definite to be clouds. To sum up, the objects described were in the shape of flying saucers. I remarked that those objects must have been really significant to him as he had felt the need to have a sister who appeared, at least in a dream, to mention those facts. All in all, the fact that he had had that dream and that he had remembered it was quite meaningful and, since the dream belonged to him, the girl reflected an aspect of his personality. Of course, he also agreed with me on this point. He later mentioned that it was remarkable how often in the midst of a clear day, there appeared some clouds—it would start to rain and everything was spoiled.

The patient went on talking about this topic, but I will not elaborate on it. I will just say that I felt he wanted me to make an interpretation of the two objects that had attacked him during that walk and which would jeopardise his relationship with his girlfriend; this also included me in the analysis. I understood that these objects would destroy the relationship if he had a real girlfriend. Once more, the patient accepted my interpretation.

As I pointed out earlier, this kind of session had become typical in the last year; I seemed to be giving excellent interpretations which were enthusiastically welcomed by the patient. Yet, by that time, I had begun to grow weary of these wonderful sessions—they didn't seem to have any effect. At the same time, I was beginning to feel irritated.

Indeed, I am accustomed to having this described as a countertransference reaction, a description with which I agree, but experience has led me to believe that it is highly improbable that one day we will see an analysis in which we cannot find any level of countertransference. The important point is this: we are told we can make use of countertransference, but I believe that, from a technical point of view, this is a mistaken concept, since, in my opinion, the term "countertransference" should be reserved for an unconscious response. For all these reasons, I believe that the alleged consciousness the analyst has of its being a countertransference is unimportant in so far as nothing can be done about it in the course of the session. Perhaps, something might be done in an instance when it comes to our own analysis; otherwise, we can just regret it. In spite of such conflicts, we must continue our work as analysts, and we must try to heal as many people as we can. We must hope to be reasonably free of those conflicts, whatever the meaning of this is. Worrying about countertransference doesn't make any sense, since, unfortunately, if we are dealing with a conscious reason we cannot do anything about it: you cannot turn to your own analyst in the midst of a session with your own patient.

Hence, I work on the principle that it is not so much a countertransference but a transference we are dealing with, in the sense that my annoyance is justified by reasons which I would consider to be conscious, or which, at least, should be conscious. Either way, the unconscious is unimportant here. This does not imply that we do not need any more analysis; it would be really difficult to make such a statement at any time, but the truth is that, no matter whether you like the idea or not, there comes a moment in which you must stop analysing yourself, and hope that the treatment you have carried out is sufficient. You must understand that, in psychoanalysis, there is a conscious participation, that, like any other job, an analysis is a task carried out in a conscious manner and that, inevitably, as a consequence of our work as psychoanalysts, we tend to develop prejudice. All kinds of reasons support the importance of the unconscious, and, as a consequence, we tend to forget that the conscious is even more important, especially for the psychoanalyst while analysing.

Now I would like to go back a bit and examine the problem of free association. Using the case described here as an example, I believe that, broadly speaking, the patient speaks, associates, and one wishes that he would do that through the use of well-structured sentences and ordinary language, and generally, this is what happens. At the same time, you receive, or expect to receive, all kinds of impressions. I believe interpretation is what is fundamental. As soon as an interpretation is made, this becomes important because it is fundamental for the patient to know what the interpretation is. Yet, when it comes to the analyst, we realise that the work that has enabled us to give that interpretation has been carried out throughout the preceding days, months, or years.

However, when I give a patient an interpretation—such as the one I have described—I trust that from the part of his communication that I have interpreted, I have also gathered a series of impressions which I have not interpreted and which I would be unable to interpret since I do not know their meaning. Yet, I do hope that—as I usually say—one day they will evolve, that is, I hope they will reach a point in which they become preconscious, conscious, and then susceptible to formulation. That point I would define as the future of the past and the present of an interpretation to come. In my opinion, this is just a typical example of the many experiences that have led me to carefully reflect about what one interprets. We run the risk of interpreting what the patient says, something the patient does not take long to perceive, and then he just starts saying things that can be subjected to interpretation.

For instance, let's take anxiety into consideration. Nobody, absolutely anybody, entertains any doubt of its reality. As analysts, we have no doubts as to what anxiety means either—we have a complete lexicon for it. However, it does not take long for this common-sense-based knowledge to lose all trace of its common sense. It does not have to do with common sense, since people have not gone through the same experience as a person trained as an analyst. What I mean is that when you are before an audience consisting of analysts, you find no difficulty in speaking about anxiety, since everybody knows well what that means. This goes beyond the limits of the analysis, though not so much as we would like to believe. What we are applying is common sense, which can also be used by other people who also have intuition too, even if their intuition has not been augmented by psychoanalytic treatment. Therefore, an analyst does not find any difficulty in assessing that an apparently hostile or enraged patient is in truth suffering from anxiety.

However, not many lay people, lacking in intuition, would accept that statement, so one easily surpasses the limits of psychoanalytic common sense. What I would like to stress here is how fast we forget that, in fact, we have much more experience than lay people, because of all the practice carried out after we finish our training. It has taught us how little we know, and that tends to have a negative effect on our analytic work. Thus, we have to take into account that, in spite of everything, we do have some knowledge; it might not be much, but still, we do have some.

This leads me to the next statement: I believe we should feel comfortable with this reality, according to which we do not need to harbour any doubt about things like anxiety, which lacks colour and, in short, is not accessible to the senses. Hence, we need to develop what I call intuition. As analysts, we find ourselves in difficulty at this point since this term has not been used before. We cannot make up a new language, and when we use the usual language and we utter something like, for example, "intuition", everybody seems to believe what we mean, but that is not true. Psychoanalysts do understand it; they have their reasons to know it because they use it at work on a daily basis. Thus, even though I use this term, I understand that we analysts use it in a special way, which is similar to the way lay people do.

I hope to have made it clear that, in a way that is unmistakable for us, we are dealing with an external reality. That is, the analyst faces an external reality of an unusual kind. In my opinion, we cannot deny that we are dealing with a reality that is virtually impossible to convey to anybody else but the patient. He enjoys an unfair advantage, so to say, as he is there and that enables him to understand it when we say: "You are feeling really anxious." Notwithstanding his decision to do it or not, he has the chance to perceive it. Yet, that is not the same when I tell somebody else. Let's take the audience here, for instance, if we ignored the fact that you are all analysts, there is no reason why you would accept that this statement is true, as the evidence I base my statement on, is not here. That evidence existed when I made that interpretation to the patient, and that is the reason why the interpretations that are effective and which the patient would not oppose are in turn criticised by our colleagues. Indeed, they do not do so out of malice, they have their reasons to do so because the lateral communication is really poor. If the object is there, one can spot it; yet, if it is not present in the analysis, it is impossible to do so.

However, I hope you will undoubtedly feel relieved to know that I have finally reached the starting point of my work. I would like to point out that I feel it is of the utmost importance to understand that our difficulties start once the analytic training has been completed. That's what I feel now, and I am afraid that is how you will feel. But I cannot make things seem easier than they really are, as I would be speaking about something completely different. However, I want to start with an approximate translation of an extract from a letter from Freud to Lou Andreas-Salomé, dated 25 May 1916. Unfortunately, I do not have it here with me, but I hope not to distort it too much. Anyway, as somebody said when speaking about philosophy, I am not writing the history of psychoanalysis, but merely taking advantage of any experience to speak about psychoanalysis on this occasion and to practise psychoanalysis on any other occasion. Freud says:

> I cannot always follow you because there are things you understand that I do not, I can appreciate their value. Partly, that is due to the fact that when I am dealing with an issue and I reach a point which is very dark, I must blind myself artificially to focus all the light on that dark spot.
>
> *Letters of Sigmund Freud*, edited by E. L. Freud (New York: Dover, 1992, pp. 312–313)

I believe we could take other aspects of this statement into consideration, but I'd rather not do it tonight. Yet, I would like to draw your attention to this point, since I deem it is extremely important for any analyst to be able to blind themselves, in the sense of relinquishing all those things that shed light, or seem to do so, upon the analytical situation. Nevertheless, this implies that when the situation becomes particularly obscure, you do not rush to find an adequate interpretation. I find it difficult to explain what I mean by this, but I hope you will eventually understand it and take some advantage of what I mean to expound here.

First of all, in my opinion, it is essential for any analyst to try to keep in their repetoire, a few essential theories. That is, a few theories felt to be essential for them and for nobody else, theories that are as popular and scarce as possible and that range over the widest field possible, because wasting time thinking about an interpretation during the analysis is not worth it; time is too valuable here. The fifty minutes that make up an ordinary session are too valuable, they are your only opportunity to obtain the material that will enable you to give an interpretation. There is nothing more important than this. This means that the analyst must stay in a condition that allows him to apprehend as much as possible. I repeat once again that I accept the need for an analytical training, but I am referring here to the development of the technique itself after your training. This means that one must know those few theories in depth.

For example, it is essential for us to be absolutely sure that we understand perfectly well what Freud meant when he spoke about the Oedipus complex. And when that has become a part of oneself, it is not necessary to make an effort to remember it, we can let it develop, without needing to rush in its search. You will have noticed that when you are feeling tired, or puzzled, you tend to rush to certainty, and an easy way to do so is by trying to find an interpretation that you feel would be blessed by some psychoanalytical pope or other.

Yet, according to my experience, it is possible to establish quite accurate categories in a certain easy way, or so I hope, with regard to some mental phenomena that intervene and tend to have a particularly darkening effect. They stand between the analyst and the reality he must get in contact with. Generally speaking, I want to use—and, in fact, I tend to use them—the terms "memory" and "desire" to refer to most of those phenomena. For instance, if the session is about to finish, I believe that one starts wondering when that moment will come; the same thing can be applied to the week and to what one will do after that session. This is precisely what desire means to me. Nevertheless, those ideas place an especially opaque screen between the analyst and the reality he must be handling in that moment.

When I say memory and desire, I am using nouns but I mean for them to have a past and a future. By way of example, in this sense it is not really important if you start wondering: "What did that patient say yesterday?" or "What am I going to do this weekend?". They are just the same thing, they share an identical quality and the same degree of opacity. While you are wondering all those things, the analysis continues and you are not really there.

You will have observed that I have changed the core of these remarks which was initially focused on the patient and the interpretations I tried to offer him, and I have moved on now to speak about the analyst. This does not mean that I want to leave the patient aside but that I feel that once we have completed our analytical training to the best of our ability, it is essential to avoid bad habits that tend to take us back to our original stage when we started our analysis as patients. Hence, I believe that it is convenient to acquire and maintain good habits in the course of our work which, in the end, takes up a considerable part of our time and regulates a great part of it.

Nonetheless, the approach that I want to emphasise here, which consists of casting a penetrating dark ray and focusing on a dark spot, presents some disappointing flaws for the analyst. I do not find it unusual since even when it comes to something as simple as learning to play tennis, if you follow the instructions given by your coach, you won't play very well, and you will resent it until it comes to be part of yourself. This can also be applied to this specific attempt to establish a close quite accurate categories relation with the realities the psychoanalyst must face.

At some point, most people feel their analysis would go very well if they could get rid of their analyst, and, on the other hand, we feel we would be excellent analysts if we could get rid of our patients. Yet, the experience I am referring to emphasises the disagreeable quality that is precisely opposed to this. Taking into account the possibility of being somehow successful, the emotional aspect of the analysis is incredibly emphasised, and I believe it is just fair to say that you get near to what Melanie Klein described, that is, the transition from the paranoid-schizoid to the depressive position. Yet, I do not believe that applying such terms in this context is convenient, just as I do not think it is useful to believe that we are free of such mechanisms. So I have tried to take for granted, and I hope I have not exaggerated, the mental balance of the psychoanalyst, and I have tried to use two other terms, paranoid-schizoid and depressive, to refer to the patient, and in return, "sufferer/patient" and "certain/safe" to refer to the analyst. I use the term "sufferer/patient" because, in English, it means both to endure frustration and to suffer, and the term "certain/safe" because it has the double meaning of free of danger and of worries. I feel them to be more pious hopes than precise descriptions, but I also feel that speaking of paranoid-schizoid and depressive is a more depressing than accurate description, so I'd rather make up these other two terms. Always assessing the issue from the point of view of the analyst, I believe that it would be hard to find a better description of the paranoid-schizoid position, in the way I am referring to it right now, than that offered by Henri Poincaré when he remarks on his experience in connection with the development of a mathematical equation. It is interesting because it lies beyond psychoanalysis and, in spite of my enormous respect for her, I do not consider Melanie Klein to have been a talented writer. On the contrary, Poincaré is a talented writer, and he portrays a situation in which he must confront a mass of phenomena that does not show any kind of resemblance that he can discern; these phenomena lack meaning and then result in a situation the human brain finds difficult to cope with. Once found, the mathematical formula and the outcome that it introduced bring order to where there was none, meaning to where it did not exist, and make apparent a relation and a coherence that were previously non-existent.

Yet, I gather that must be our attitude towards the analytical situation. On encountering the patient again, the following day, it is essential for this patient to be no longer the patient we knew but somebody we have never seen before. However, this is not an easy task; it is not easy to get rid of memories, and it might be better this way. The important point here is that a new situation must be appreciated. If something has already been interpreted, it has already fulfilled its purpose. When that material emerges again, it will have a different appearance. Hence, we need not worry about what we have already said, or about what the patient has previously said, we just need to worry about what is happening at that moment. Neither yesterday nor the previous day, tomorrow is important. If the material is relevant, it will come up again in the evolution, as I call it, of the interpretations. It will arise and it will occupy its proper place, like the image on the television screen. Its appearance will not be similar to when we remember a dream, but to when one says: "Ah, that reminds me I had a dream!" The dream emerges like a whole; that is what I understand by evolution. If you remember it, it appears in a fragmented way, little by little, and nobody knows what those fragments mean.

The patient cannot cooperate in this sense. The patient tends to arrive and say: "Don't you recognise me? I am the same depression, the same anxiety, that you met yesterday and the day before, and we will continue meeting in years to come." In my opinion, to ourselves we should say: "Go away. Today I am welcoming a new patient, and if you want me to, I will introduce him to you."

Nevertheless, there are certain compensations, as at least it reduces the burden of those terrible analyses that go on forever and never change, which always offer the same cooperation, the same dreams; in short, all those things that indicate that we are always dealing with the same patient. I have already pointed out the negative side to this.

As far as I'm concerned, I believe I will never be able to get rid of that slight feeling of persecution I experience when I have to face a situation that I do not understand. I'd rather keep a situation I do understand, and the patient would be more than willing to comfort me, something he would achieve by providing me with the material that would lead me to believe that I am dealing with the same person I saw yesterday, the day before, or last year. Nevertheless, I deem it is important to examine these unfathomable, unrelated, and incoherent situations, instead of devoting ourselves to the understandable, coherent ones. The latter are unimportant, there is nothing to discover about them anymore. We have to focus, so to speak, on unfathomable, incoherent, and unrelated facts.

This feeling of impatience, as I would describe it in an elegant way, or of persecution, to be more direct, is of such a nature that one yearns to put an end to it by finding an interpretation, or by remembering an interpretation, if possible. This is precisely what we must resist. The patient will not like it and you will not like it either, but I feel it is necessary to focus on the incoherent situation until it becomes coherent, in other words, until we reach the depressive position, the secure position.

Indeed, this has been my aim in mentioning this problem regarding both the analyst and the patient: I want to refer now to the fact that the further you advance towards your aim of becoming an analyst, the nearer you are to replacing your own analyst with the patient. I do not mean to say that one is analysed by the patients themselves; that may happen, but this is just part of the material used for the interpretations. What I mean to say is that in our work patients occupy now a significant position, it is so important that it has an effect on our emotional life that does not differ completely from the effect our own analyst has.

Some similarities can be found: one of them is that, if you manage to follow the path I am suggesting here, I can promise you a life full of feelings of persecution or of depression. It is a somewhat extreme way to put it, but I believe you will find that you tend to attribute those feelings of patience or of security to situations which, in truth, belong to the analytic work itself. The peculiarity of all this, supposing that in the course of a session you have been lucky enough to make two or three coherent interpretations, which resemble a pattern and a meaning, is that it is surprising to see how frequently you feel depressed at the end of that session. And you will see that that situation turns negative and is in need of a theory in itself. At this point I am referring exactly to that theory.

I am mentioning this point since I consider that it is an important example of how to face our work and that it is also what makes our task so hard. I also feel it is the reason why our work is so valuable but, at the same time, the reason why so many casualties occur among us. It is just natural for vacancies to occur among what could be called a psychoanalytical group if we bear in mind that we are dealing with something so terrible as the human mind. That implies that apart from the analytical training, it is fundamental to have a good approach, or at least to try to have one. As aforementioned, difficulties appear precisely when you have already completed your training; so, the problem regarding the way in which you approach your own work, your state of mind, appears once you complete your own analysis and once the analyst cannot continue being analysed.

Question 1

About the way in which the analyst comes to understand and establish those few theories that must make up his therapeutic arsenal; the questioner points out that Dr Bion seems to consider analytical work to be arduous, while not taking into account its stimulating aspects at the same time.

Dr Bion: To my understanding, every analyst should maintain a sense of proportion and admit the insignificant role they play within a much wider movement. I do not see much merit in the ability I have—and which other people do not have—to convey things in a penetrating way. I have tried to say this same thing at the British Psychoanalytic Society on numerous occasions; this means, if people examine what I say they will not find anything original in my words, in fact, they will ascertain it as soon as they realise it is something they already knew. But the important point here is that, just in the same way as parents who repeat the same thing once and over again until, in the end, that evident truth they were trying to convey becomes clear to us and we say: "Ah, that is what they meant", the same thing can happen in the analysis: one repeats the same thing once and over again until, one day, people say: "Ah, that is what it meant". I do not consider I have discovered anything new, since I understand that one must admit that on certain occasions what has been often repeated suddenly appears to be original. Undoubtedly, this has to do with yourself, and also with the moment it is said, and with the background of those listening. I do not think I am exaggerating if I say that this can even be applied to Freud. Everybody used to say: "Well, we knew all that about sex even before he started to deal with this issue", something Freud himself pointed out in some of his works, but the fact that the rest of them didn't say it, at least not in the same way, was the starting point of it all.

[Response to Dr Pichon-Riviere's remark]: I want to thank Dr Pichon-Riviere for his remarks and I would like to say that it was very pleasing that someone reminds me of the old Society in which Dr Rickman was also a participant. I consider it is really interesting to hear somebody remind us of the historical development of which we're just a piece; I am not surprised at all to realise that one draws some kind of circle that takes you back to work that has already been done. One hopes to be able to add something new to it and also to be able to relive and to give it the relevance it merits again. It is undeniable that many important things are said, which are then forgotten and then remain buried, in their slumber, until someone brings them back to life again. This is characteristic of the history of science, not just peculiar to psychoanalysis; however, I feel we must be aware of this fact, and we must be willing to appreciate and greet our predecessors who made a contribution to psychoanalysis which, even if it might be forgotten for a while, will inevitable reappear, with renewed vitality.

Question 2

If the question of leaving aside the historical factors of the analysis will result in an increase in your internal perception, and if the use of that internal perception sustains the use of intuition over the basis of the clarifying darkness mentioned by Bion.

Dr Bion: Indeed. I believe that that is exactly the case. I did not mention the unpleasant aspect inherent in the attempt at getting rid of all memory and desire, but it can be observed in an extreme case, in the psychotic patient who ingeniously manages to get rid of the stimuli originating from reality, because he finds them unbearable, and believes he will get to avoid them through withdrawal, if there is a regression to what, lacking in a better term, we must call the unconscious, that is to his own interior self.

Nevertheless, this is not what you try to achieve, you hope that with the development of the analysis you will be able to—as Freud puts it-artificially blind yourself, with a genuine affect, without its resulting in something like a total regression, what, evidently, would be disastrous in any analysis. Unfortunately, it is also true that when a deeply psychotic patient is analysed, the analyst can, by emphasising the existence of his unconscious motivation, lead him to free himself of the conflict by the method of getting rid of conscience, and, as a result, the sanity that he might have had before will disappear and the analyst will encounter a real psychotic, not to mention the psychotic's family. As a result, it is important to emphasise the conscious aspect of what the patient says when dealing with cases like these. As mentioned before, you do not obviously try to do things like these unless you are sure you are deeply acquainted, so to say, with the domain of mental life. In that case, I understand you feel less intimidated by the weird and disagreeable experiences you will probably have to endure. Yet, the patient is not familiar with this, and I think that danger is real.

To my mind, this has to do with what Dr Rodrigué stated about the need to keep the capacity for memory and desire; I am afraid what I said could lead you to mistakenly understand that I think that the analyst benefits from maiming his personality, something which is not true. I think it is important for the analyst to live and to keep his ability to lead an ordinary life, which includes things like memory and desire, either for happy experiences or for hopes or future plans, which makes everything even more difficult. All in all, I still believe that what I have said is very important—otherwise, I would not have made you waste your time—but I do not know if the price to pay is your own personality. I think analysts must train in that sense and keep the ability to get rid of memory and desire as part of their role as analysts. There are no easy problems to solve, even less so "in bulk", so to say, which is implicit when you say that you have to get rid of memory and desire. It is something that has to do with a precise task, which might be a very important task in our lives as analysts, but never at the expense of our own personality. What's more, I believe that is one of the reasons why the psychotic falls apart is precisely his "in bulk" way to lose touch with reality.

SECOND SEMINAR

The nature of internal and external objects—the psychoanalytical model of Melanie Klein—projective identification—theory of container/contained—the mystic and the Establishment—Science and Christianity—audience questions

Today, I want to speak about a matter which, in spite of not having to do with psychoanalytic theory but with psychoanalytic observation instead, is of the utmost importance to me, since, as I have previously said, I believe failure is once and again either the result of the impossibility to observe clearly or the consequence of an inability to pass on to others the received impression.

I do not believe that the understanding of psychoanalytic theory related to internal and external objects presents much difficulty; reviewing the relevant literature with the aim of making your own selection might be a very useful exercise—especially the works of Melanie Klein and Freud. However, the issue of identifying the internal and external objects while dealing with the patient in the office is much more important and not so easy to convey to others, because in clinical examples we are offered the description of a specific case, and each specific case always seems to be very different from others. Thus, there exists an abundance of specific cases and a tendency to believe that we need a different theory to deal with each of them.

However, the ultimate aim of any science is to simplify a theory as much as possible and, at the same time, to design a theory capable of containing as many particular cases as possible. Thus, what I mean to do is to bridge this gap—the existing gap we perceive during the analysis between theory and the patient. To this aim, I intend to start off with two symbols—the male symbol and the female symbol—in the way they are used in biology, but I'd rather refer to them as the container and contained, so as to provide them with a wider meaning than that generally applied to gender symbols.

One of the earliest situations in which Melanie Klein put into practice this specific idea is related to the theory of projective identification. She proposed that the baby splits parts of itself off and projects them onto its mother's breast—the breast is the most primitive version of this theory—and so it can later recover them. Hence, if the infant is suffering from anxiety, they can split it off and project it on to the mother, so to speak—have their omnipotent fantasy, since that is what it is—and then get it back when it has apparently been detoxified—that is, when it has become less frightening.

On one occasion, three or four colleagues and myself were examining a case that was causing trouble to one of us; at that point, I suggested to Melanie Klein that the case would not offer any difficulty, that is, what is usually known as a negative therapeutic reaction, if we bore in mind that it is possible to combine several theories, the theory of projective identification and, especially, the theory that maintains that the baby projects what he cannot cope with and then gets it back when it has undergone a process of detoxification, with the theories she was working on at the time, related to envy and gratitude.

At this point, I would like to refer to models. Models are just imaginary stories, created with the aim of their having some sort of psychological effect on us, in the sense of their helping us to have some knowledge of the theory, an even more abstract knowledge, which, nevertheless, keeps a recognisable distance from what we can face in the office. First of all, I would like to offer a model for a failed projective identification which, according to our theories, follows a certain course and is a source of unhappiness for the patient. The baby feels scared of dying and cries. The mother reacts with anxiety and says: "I don't know what's wrong with this baby", and tends to distance herself from the crying baby, either in reality or psychologically, by not being willing to calm the baby down. This is a model of the situation in which the baby has split a part of itself off—its fear of dying—and it cries to project it onto the mother but that part is rejected and projected again onto the child. As aforementioned, the model is: "I don't know what's wrong with this baby", and also anxiety and impatience as an answer.

Now, as a model for a successful projective identification, let's imagine an affectionate and motherly type of normal woman and a baby who also cries because it is afraid of dying. The mother takes the baby in her arms, smiles with affection, and says: "It's alright, it's alright, it's no big worry", and a few seconds later the baby is also smiling and accepts being placed back in the cradle. According to the theory, this is a model where the baby splits off its fear of death, and as I suggested, it projects it on to its mother's breast, the mother detoxifies it, and the baby gets back a slight fear. However, let's say that for some reason or other the affectionate loving mother is not there, either because she doesn't love her baby or because she is suffering from some kind of anxiety, or maybe because the baby is especially disturbed and is afraid of its mother, that is, the kind of thing that would happen with a psychotic baby. In the model for that situation, we could say that the baby feels fear because it feels that it is dying, splits off that fear and projects it on to its mother's breast but, in this case, we guess there is some kind of hostility, either in the mother or in the baby, which spoils the omnipotent phantasy and prevents the breast from detoxifying the fear. Here we have the feeling that that bad object strips away the projections of the baby from the meaning they could have had in an avid, envious, and hostile way. Thus the fear of dying that the baby feels can be projected on to the maternal breast, when the baby gets it back, it has been turned into a nameless dread; in other words, what was projected on to the mother's breast—the fear of dying—has even been stripped of the meaning it had and has just become, as I said before, a nameless dread. These are three completely imaginary situations; I have no idea of what a baby thinks and I don't think I ever will, it only remains for each of us to imagine our own version. But the important thing about these three pictorial examples is that they provide us with some kind of visual image that allows us to understand such an abstract theory a bit better.

I would like to offer now some other examples of what, in essence, is the same problem, of whatever these two symbols represent, female and male, container and contained, as I have called them, with the aim, as I mentioned before, of making them even more abstract. On the one hand, we could consider the existence of language, which has been adapted, whose vocabulary has corresponding meanings, thanks to which each word has a definition and can be found in a dictionary. This is a fixed situation; those words, at least in theory, have a meaning that should not be modified. If this were true, there would exist no development in language. Using dictionaries and attributing existing words their correct meaning is reasonable; I want to highlight this because I will come back to this point. Not only a baby or an infant but also an adult, all of us, can have something to communicate and find ourselves in the situation of the baby who uses an unknown form of language: it can use its crying, which possesses a vast number of meanings, some of which we can understand while others we can't. But I want to make reference to something more abstract, that is, to a situation in which the attempt to convey a meaning is carried out through language and there arises a kind of conflict between the language that is a container and the meaning, which is the assumed contained object. If the vocabulary is firm and it is well established, when you project on it an unusual meaning, because that is the point, something that the speaker or the creator of the idea wants to convey as a novelty, it is expressed in such rigid or limited words that the resulting statement strips the meaning of all life. I am using this metaphorical language in a deliberate way.

Let's take into consideration now a term such as infant sexuality, or adolescent sexuality. Indeed, it is very easy to establish the meaning of these words: infant or adolescent sexuality. If the people taking part in a conversation in which these terms are being used are hostile, then such words will not convey a meaning, they will strip it of all life instead. Such statements do not have any meaning, because it has been murdered by the container, that is, by the words, and by the speaker who uses them as well. But if words are allowed to be used in such a way that they become suitable containers for the ideas placed in them, then it is possible to reach the proliferation of this idea in the vast psychoanalytic literature regarding infant and adolescent sexuality. Then the idea can possibly be extended, without causing language any harm. For the uninformed, everything is the same: envy, gratitude, sex, everybody knows what they mean, but they do not know what they mean to the analysts.

Let's imagine there is something wrong with the baby. It is trying to express something, something it needs; the baby whimpers and finally cries. Let's suppose that, at a subsequent stage, it does not want to cry and so on, and prefers to express itself through language; but here feelings are also so intense that unless we are dealing with a child who speaks very well, who is particularly fluent, it will be extremely difficult for him to find a way to express himself. As a result, either language explodes or we find ourselves in the kind of situation that corresponds to a patient who offers countless free associations, and suddenly says "I am afraid I am going to commit suicide", and continues with another series of free associations. This is a situation in which language is used to strip very powerful emotions of all life. In truth, all the series of associations say very little when it comes to expressing or communicating the fear of suicide; in short, they constitute a communication that tends to go unnoticed by the analyst precisely because it tends to strip of all life what the patient wants to say in reality, instead of conveying all the strength in what he wants to state. To my mind, the danger of these situations lies in the fact that the nature of the associations leads us not to worry much, not to pay special attention precisely to that which remains hidden, and suddenly the patient commits suicide, apparently without any previous warning.

Up to this point, I have dealt specifically with verbal communication since it is true that we attribute enormous significance to it, as we use it so often in analysis; but the important aspect of this type of model resides in the fact that we can count on it in a way—for example, when somebody stutters—that allows us to consider the possibility, as I already mentioned to some of you, of a case in which the important thing was not so much what the patient said at a certain point—I am not referring to all the treatment or to the peculiar characteristics of his stuttering—but to the fact that his tongue was contained in his mouth. That was the important and significant point. I do not want to waste any time by going back to this case, but I do want to add that everything that followed that moment is nothing but absolutely conventional analytic theory, there is nothing original in it, absolutely nothing.

As I stated earlier, it is not my intention to increase an already abundant psychoanalytic literature, as I believe that the output of the great psychoanalysts is more than enough for us to get along. What I do want to highlight is: please, try to identify it in the office, with the patient; and also try to obtain different versions of these theories that have this kind of abstract quality, the container and the contained. That might alert you to the point when you will start to understand that the significant factor in a problem such as stuttering, which we seem to be unable to modify, does not lie in oral communication and so on, but in this other possibility: that there exists a relation between the tongue and the mouth and, as you will remember, the rest of the food canal. I am just mentioning this because I intend to continue with the topic of oral communication and I want to suggest that, if you are interested, you should create your own models, just take the female and male symbols and then invent your own toys of this kind, so as to gain some practice, not to enrich analytic theory but as a way to practise the construction of models.

At this point, I would like to make a sort of leap towards the other model, because I do not want to waste much time on these models that have to do with theories that, in truth, cannot express a certain idea that has precisely arisen thanks to these theories. A new formulation is required in order to incorporate it. In physics, for instance, if we take into consideration something like the theory of the expansion of gases, several modifications become necessary, we need to introduce new ideas that allow us to extend the theory so as to make it more suitable for subtler observations. This happens all the time, and here it can also be understood in terms of the container which must adapt itself to the contained object or vice versa. The same kind of model can be applied to determine if the analysis takes place in the office, under the analyst's observation, or outside the office, which is known in English as "no acting out"—I do not know how the same idea can be expressed in Spanish. What really interests me is not oral communication as such, but the fact that there is something known as "acting out" which expresses a similar idea, that of a container of the analysis and the problem regarding whether it is really contained or not.

However, I would always like to refer to the same topic, to the same invariability implied here, the messianic idea, the messianic person, the genius, the mystic, or all those terms used to designate the same object. That specific phenomenon I want to refer to also appears in science, in Newton, for example; it appears in religion, with the mystics—I do not relate to Christian religion in any specific way, but to any religion in which the mystics always seem to live an experience that is clearly similar, regardless of their origin, their time, their religion, or their social status. I believe that when the intensity or the force reaches a certain level in the messianic idea or in the mystic—terms I will use from now on to be brief and to refer both to the idea and to the person—that always exerts an explosive, destructive, catastrophic effect on the environment. Indeed, up to a point that depends on the environment we are dealing with. We have a term, "the Establishment", which has recently become popular in England; it does not have quite a precise meaning but it could be understood as "the authorities", that is, ecclesiastical dignitaries, members of parliament, the prime minister, and so on and so forth; to sum up, those people to whom an executive role within the state can be attributed. I believe that we can find what we call "the Establishment" in any group, no matter how small it is, and we could even say that we can also find it within the individual, in the sense that the individual itself could be represented in its diverse characteristics by the people in a group. There is a part in any individual that exercises some kind of control function. Hence we have this relationship between "the Establishment" and the mystic.

Yet, taking part and identifying oneself with one or the other is very easy, but in truth that does not take us anywhere, due to the fact that we need a Faraday to be able to enjoy electric light; there must be some kind of organisation, some "Establishment" capable of taking Faraday's discoveries and formulating the physical laws, or the laws of electricity, as we could call them, since we are not dealing with laws made by nature, but with the resulting laws of a formulation. As a consequence, we needn't bother to discover electricity if we want to light up a room: we simply need to turn on the light. And, this way, ordinary people, do not need to be Faraday in order to light up a room. The same thing applies to science: we need a Descartes or a Galileo to invent a mathematical formula that can measure growth. If that task is suitably carried out, we can obtain formulations of such scope that any student today can solve problems that once required a Galileo or a Descartes to be solved. Such formulation has now become accessible. Hence, what I mean is that "the Establishment" must be understood as something of the utmost importance, it must be understood to be as important as the mystic.

I guess that a classical example of this is one of the greatest mystics, Jesus. To my mind, in this case "the Establishment" did not handle the situation well, since they gave way to a situation where the maddening influence of Jesus over the Jewish community was so big that this community has since suffered as a consequence. The question is to find the way in which the mystic's contribution—Jesus' contribution in this case—whichever it is, becomes accessible, and, in spite of it, the group survives. In truth, this situation was a failure, as it meant the unhinging of the Jewish community, and the role of control, of acting as an "Establishment" to face Jesus' messianic ideas, was assumed by what would later become the Christian hierarchy. After Jesus' death, the messianic ideas kept their disturbing power and have remained since a source of trouble, especially for the Christian hierarchy, who in their attempt to keep a mystic's ideas under control—on the countless occasions on which those ideas would explode—had to take responsibility for the problems related to heresy etc. Whether these kinds of ideas have eventually been put back on track or not is subject to opinion; many people understand that we live in a more civilised world thanks to Jesus' teachings. But under any circumstances, we must bear in mind that there has always existed this conflict between the "Establishment" and the surviving ideas. The conflict between whether it is possible to deprive Jesus' teachings of all meaning or if they should be allowed to drive society to despair: that is the question. In this context, it is really interesting to read a primitive synoptic gospel like the Gospel according to Mark, and to observe the strange conjunction of certain characteristics.

At this point, I would like to remark upon another correspondence: the equivalent of what could be considered the scientific laws in a scientific approach to this issue, would correspond to the dogma in a religious approach. The dogma is nothing else but the attempt to make certain mystic experiences accessible to the common man, a substitute for the religious experience; it is a set of rules, a substitute for electricity and magnetic attraction, that allows us to turn on the light when we so desire. The dogma is a substitute for the difficulties and unforeseen complications implicit in mysticism itself. Thus, thanks to the formulation that is a dogma, something is made accessible to the common religious person.

I have already mentioned that Christian hierarchy inherited some very serious problems related to the fact of containing Jesus, so to speak. I am using the word "contain" here in the same sense as it is used by the army in expressions such as "contain a fortress": that is, to surround a fortress with troops so that those inside the fortress cannot leave it. The other side to this within the Jewish community is the possession of a greater knowledge of how to control people as, for example, in the case of Isaac Luria, who never wrote down a word but who preached, taught everything he had to say, as, according to him, it was an indescribable experience impossible to express in a written work. In Spain, this situation was dealt with by the Jewish hierarchy in a much more efficient way, as their acts did not provoke a population uprising and did not lead to the loss of Isaac Luria's teachings. It is undoubtedly a very interesting issue. I believe that the Christian hierarchy inherited the problem that messianic ideas imply and that the Jews who inherited an identical problem, either in a conscious or unconscious way, had to learn the knowledge taught by their rabbis. To my mind, one of the important factors in this question is the understanding of the messianic idea which, as far as I know, has never been really well understood, except perhaps by extremely specialised Jewish organisations who really understand what this idea means.

I would like to make a parenthetical remark here to explain how these facts are described, for example in the Gospel according to Mark—this early synoptic gospel. It is especially noteworthy that, even though in appearance we are dealing with a religious phenomenon, or, at least, with a phenomenon generally applied in a religious sense, that in the Gospel according to Mark, they speak about what an extraordinary person Jesus was, about how people were amazed by this and so on, but what Jesus preached is mentioned further on. What this gospel offers is nothing but tales about all those people who approached him in search of healing. As I said, this is noteworthy because when reading the gospel, we find a constant conjunction of the different features, and one is led to believe that there must exist in it a discernible pattern that includes a certain stimulus which brings about a group of phenomena such as the demand for healing, the expectation of a miracle, the concept of a religious or philosophical treatment, and, what's more, the announcement of some kind of paradise or new world. Indeed, taking into consideration which concepts come together under certain historical circumstances would be worth it. Yet, the failure of the key figure, as I call it, to live up to such expectations provokes an extremely hostile response; in fact, one of the primitive responses might be appreciated every day, that is, the concept that God is there to be beaten any time our absurd demands are not satisfied. And I believe this to be one of the analyst's roles as well: no matter how absurd a patient's demands, what really matters to them is not so much a wish to be healed but to have someone to crush because they have not done what they wanted.

Nietzsche stated that the role of a nation was to produce a genius, you need all the population in a country to achieve it, and that is their function. Whether we agree with that statement or not, I believe that it is an extreme stance that can be taken, and I would even say that our function as psychoanalysts or as a psychoanalytic society consists in setting up the kind of "Establishment" which would allow, if we were lucky enough to count on some geniuses, so that they could exist in a society such as today's. In other words, the function of the container consists in that case in letting growth take place. Yet, as usual, we come across the same situation: if envy, hatred, rivalry, and so on are predominant, the new idea as well as its creator will be crushed; if we take the opposite stance, the new idea or its creator will derange the whole society. The question here is how to contain that explosion. I believe that this is a very elaborate description of this special concept of the container and contained, but I mean to use it as a model for one of the many variations on the same issue, to get you to understand what I mean to describe by using these simple symbols of female and male for the container and the contained. The predominant emotional state determines what the relation will be between both objects within a wide range of circumstances and variety of formulations. I had better leave it here and start answering the thousands of questions that you are probably willing to put to me.

Question 1

I would like to know if the main factor in those derangements is an increase in the feelings of paranoia; could we consider that the "Establishment" corresponds to the secondary process?

Dr Bion: No, I would not make such a division, because these messianic objects, these geniuses, etc. must be contained by ordinary groups and by ordinary people. Let's take, for example, that Freud had thought that he was Freud. Just imagine how terrible believing that he was Freud might have been, together with the gradual discovery that indeed he was so. I find it impossible to imagine because I am not Freud, but what matters is that he had enough courage to behave as if he were Freud much earlier than anybody who would ever hear of him. I assume that this is one of the requisites, that is, that the individual must tolerate what seems to be a megalomaniacal idea. But that courage must be extended to the group as well, to the society, to the container which grows wider and wider; it must be capable of containing the genius, in the same way as the genius must be able to contain its own genius.

I believe it depends to a great extent on who judges whether it is a megalomaniacal idea or not; obviously it depends on the individual. The fear of progress of the individual can prevent growth and it is related to this fear of megalomania, whatever that is; psychiatrists and analysts attribute some meaning to this term, but probably so does the individual even before they have come across this word. As far as I am concerned, the difficulty lies in the fact that the person who would be recognised as a genius, and not only within their family, constitutes such an exceptional and strange case that it is highly improbable that we might be able to study them or that they might seek analytical treatment. Yet this raises an odd question with regard to the sharp characteristic of the genius: the effect that it has beyond a certain environment. If we take into consideration a schizophrenic patient, for example, their relation is extremely intense but very limited; in fact, it does not go beyond their own skin. But if we take into account the case of a genius, it becomes apparent that it goes beyond their family, their motherland, and probably beyond their time. This is clearly appreciated in one of the Odes by Horace—I do not remember well which one it is, but it is found in Book IV—in which we are told that there existed brave men before Agamemnon, but we did not need a Homer to tell us so, we know of Agamemnon and his deeds. I cannot call to mind the exact quotation, but in general terms that is its meaning. In other words, we find ourselves in a situation in which a man is of such nature, and I am referring to Homer here, that he can make his ideas pervade many centuries after his death. Shakespeare, in turn, expresses this same idea.

[Comments on the importance Dr Bion attributes to intuition when working with the patient]: I find this comment very interesting and it makes me more convinced that this Society seems to be favourable to this approach. I believe it constitutes the basis for any effective work and that one of the biggest difficulties will reside in making the analytic movement stay in the hands of those who practise it instead of in the hands of those whose only intention is to speak about the topic and who have their own ulterior motives to adopt that attitude. I believe that we always run the risk of losing control of the psychoanalytic movement. I would express it this way: if psychoanalysis cannot be sustained, if it cannot be contained, then we must seize the container.

THIRD SEMINAR

The Grid as an instrument to assess deterioration as well as evolution of thinking—how the Grid is used—the Grid's use as a tool for discovering latent content—the analyst's own Grid—doubts and scepticisms about the Grid—audience questions

I would like to refer to the Grid as an instrument designed to help us in the development of our thought. Even though it is based on theories, it is not a theory itself. Indeed, it would be better described as a set of rules when working on something written. It is nothing else but a useful tool. Nevertheless, as I have drawn it, the Grid is incomplete, and if somebody found it useful they should try to enhance its usefulness on the basis of their own specific clinical experience. Yet, I find it important to highlight that, in the course of your work, you must never let thoughts of the Grid draw you from your task. To my mind, it is more useful before or after fulfilling a task, like, for example, on this occasion, because it can help us shed light on our own ideas. Indeed, I feel it is especially useful when an analyst is working on his own, without anybody to make critical remarks on his work, so that he is thus forced to be his own supervisor.

The Grid is very simple. On the vertical axis we place A, B, C, D, etc., and on the horizontal axis we place 1, 2, 3, 4, up to n. The idea is that the first letter, A, corresponding to the vertical axis, represents something that lacks in completion, though in truth, I feel it should represent something which hardly belongs to the domain of thought.

Hence, it could so be stated that the vertical axis in truth represents anything that ranges from what you cannot think at all to something different which could be defined as part of our thought, but about which we have no information. Since I consider it useful to speak about the vertical axis of the Grid, I assign a name to it, so that we can speak about it; though this does not imply that the name is meaningful. Whenever we try to do something of this sort, we usually find out that meaning interferes. This does not imply that the word is used because it has a meaning, since, from a clinical perspective, I do not believe it is possible to perceive it, no matter how much we wish to speak about it.

Generally speaking, one takes into consideration what Freud states in Chapter VII of *The Interpretation of Dreams*. Obviously, Freud worked from a different perspective, building upon the manifest content of the dream, so that he could later arrive at the latent content. Yet, I would like to describe this Grid from a different perspective. I hope I will have enough time to explain what I understand by perspectives, as these occur in analysis; it is impossible to know if we are approaching an issue from a certain point of view because it is something that has not yet been examined.

Nevertheless, from my point of view, our capacity to produce alpha-elements enables us to dream. It is just in a later stage that the dream is remembered vividly enough for the patient to be able to describe it, and this is generally done in terms most commonly applied to visual impressions. That's why I am saying that alpha-elements mark the commencement of thinking, although in truth, nothing similar can be felt in practice. It is just a way to speak about something even if we can neither feel nor find it. To give you an idea as to why I deem it useful to employ those categories that, as aforementioned, are never really found in practice: I should suggest that when you have a patient who, for example, makes a grimace, and you think that he is observing the way in which interpretations are going over his head; to be honest, I do not know how to define that. I have no idea what he is looking at. After a while, I might reach the conclusion that we were dealing with hallucinations, he might in truth be seeing something, in which case we would not speak of beta-elements, as we have a different term to describe this. But so long as we do not know what they are, it is useful to define them as beta-elements as a means to reflect upon them and even to refer to them when speaking to somebody. As I said, you can discard it, as it does not constitute a clinical condition but just something that can help us speak about something similar to this. Whether you call them thoughts or aspects of thought will, undoubtedly, depend on your own clinical experience or on what you consider to be useful. Nevertheless, in contrast with this, I would say that a patient who states: "I had a dream, but I do not remember it", is capable of alpha-elements. Once again, we will not know what they are, not even whether they exist or not, but I believe that if the patient makes that assertion, he will have entered the domain of thought, of something that can genuinely be rendered as thought.

I do not mean to deal with the remaining letters. In letter "C", I would place something like visual images, etc., and all that stuff, mythology, anything that has quite a defined sensual basis and which uses that kind of language in a descriptive way. I would like to extend it to questions that so far we cannot describe very well because language itself hasn't been—as far as I know—sufficiently developed. For instance, if the patient expresses that he has had a dream but that he is unable to remember it, this would constitute an example. But, I also believe that, especially when it comes to a specific kind of patient, it is advisable to bear in mind that it might be possible that, even though they have had a dream, the question does not lie with their inability to recall it, but in the fact that it is obviously appreciated in terms of physical sensations, of visual sensations. So the patient cannot say anything about it because he is not able to turn a muscular sensation into a verbal representation. I would like to include *all* this in category "C". In reference to the Grid, this implies that it will be necessary for those who use category "C" to widen and subdivide it, since as it stands now, it is too vague. I honestly believe we stand the chance of making it more detailed than it is today without its losing in accuracy.

I am not much interested in the remaining categories, since I consider they do not preoccupy us much, although they might be useful, for example, in physics, that is, for those interested in preconception, conception, the theoretical system, and, ultimately, in the algebraic formulation of the system, which I tend to deem extremely elaborate. All in all, if I have the time for it, I would like to approach this question from the opposite view. In a sense, it is understood that we are dealing with something really primitive. It seems to be really intricate, but in truth, its development is not sufficiently complete so as to be used in psychoanalysis. It is my intention to express it this way, because scientists tend to state that psychoanalysis is not a science because it has not been "mathematised". I would say that it *is* a science indeed, but given that scientists cannot keep up with us, they have not managed to design mathematical formulae that can be useful for us. That's the reason why we cannot use mathematics: it is not good enough for us.

Yet, the horizontal axis of the Grid refers to the use we make of formulation. Now I should explain how I interpret principle or formulation. Let's take: "Pedro", that would be a verbal formulation, but what has it been used for? For instance, I can use it to call somebody, to attract his attention. That is what I understand by "use". Or I could say the same thing but in a way that would suggest reproach; the word is the same, but the meaning is really different. And that is our challenge: we know that if we write down the word "Pedro" in an article, it does not really mean much to anybody; it represents a lack of communication among analysts, and I believe this is the root of much unnecessary controversy lacking in meaning and resulting from the enormous failure that I consider lateral communication to be.

The first column has to do with what I call Definitory Hypothesis. It has to do with things that can't be argued because they are mere definitions. If somebody defines what he is saying, there cannot exist any argument, because he is just expressing the way in which he uses language. Yet, when a person has made this statement, it is legitimate to expect him to be coherent within the limits of his definition. We need to know that words are used in that specific way and that they are not going to be continuously modified.

The second column refers to the pronouncements that are false, and whose falsifications can be known. However, this category and the others require a subdivision, which would be related to a concept taken from one of the letters written by the English poet Keats. He speaks about "negative capability" and states that it was one of Shakespeare's most precious assets. In his opinion, a language of achievement depends on negative capability. I consider it a bad description, not worth remembering at this point. Keats declares that negative capability could be defined as the ability to tolerate mysteries, half-truths, and doubts, etc. —and this is what interests me—without feeling the need to reach for certainty. I would like to base myself on the use of this conception to make a division between the language of achievement and its opposite. The crucial point here is that, in psychoanalytical practice, it is of the utmost importance to stay sharp so as to notice when the patient, while using the same words, is applying a language of achievement, which constitutes a prelude to action, or a language which represents a substitute for action, because I am positive that some analyses that appear to be endless use a language aimed at substituting action and not as a prelude to it.

Focusing on this same question from a different perspective, I would say that language of achievement possesses a quality that is particularly penetrating. Inevitably, once more we are using analogies taken from the sensory experience here. Such language pervades time and space. For that reason, Keats proved to be wise when he said that Shakespeare's language is a language of achievement, because it has pervaded every century. The same could be said of any classic writer, like Virgil, Horace, etc. They managed to find the language of achievement. Equally, for different reasons, it is of the utmost importance for analysts to be able to do the same. The fact of pervading time or space might not seem very important, but it is so if we intend to be able to convey our interpretation to the patient. Obviously, the patient will take the necessary steps in that regard, depending on his aim in that moment. Yet, even though I believe this should be reflected at some point in the Grid, it is not the case. It could be said that, in truth, in the first category, the alpha-elements, should have that pervasive quality, they should enable the patient to dream. And, as we know, dream itself can hold a possibility of achievement. To my understanding, the patient who never brings a dream, or who even claims never to dream, is telling us a lot about his ability to penetrate to the depths and about the kind of language we can expect from him.

I am afraid all this will seem to be extremely theoretical and remote from the task that you must carry out. That is not my aim and, throughout this seminar, I would like you to bear in mind that we are constantly referring to tomorrow's session, neither to yesterday's nor to the one held the day before that, but to the one we will hold tomorrow, to the one that has not taken place yet. Thus, we are all on the same footing, since I know nothing about the patient and neither do you.

The next item is this: the patient expresses that he would like to have a car or a sail boat. Among other things, what we need to know at this point is what that statement means and for what purpose it is being used. What effect does the patient expect to have when he makes such a statement to the analyst? At the same time, he is not expecting to do anything. Are we dealing with the language of achievement, with some kind of daydreaming which will, one day, lead him to take the necessary steps to obtain the car or the sail boat, or is it meant as a substitute for action, as a fantasy which will not become real? I do not believe we will be able to give an answer to this question in any particular session, thanks to any specific principle. We will be able to do so in due time, since then it will be possible to appreciate the fact that the patient is talking on with ease, that there are many free associations, many interpretations, and that he is acting as if you were not there. We are dealing then with a substitute for action. The analyst must learn to acknowledge their differences and differentiate them. I do not know how to describe this process because if it appears in a written work, the difference between each of them disappears. But, during the treatment, the difference is unmistakable once you have learned to acknowledge its existence. This is why we are here speaking about things that I would describe as indescribable. Incidentally, I would say that one of the peculiarities of analysis is that, fortunately, even if lateral communication proves to be really poor, the communication during the analytical session is not, because the interpretations must refer to something that both the patient and the analyst are experiencing. This is the reason why, on many occasions, an interpretation is obvious both for the analyst and for the patient, but cannot be understood by any other person, including our colleagues, who would wonder why the analyst is speaking such nonsense and formulating such fantastical theories. Yet if you are immersed in the analytical experience, the why is completely evident in so far as the language we are dealing with is the language of achievement and it is being used by someone who is a real psychoanalyst able to get through to somebody who has come to him in search of analytical treatment.

I believe we should pause here so that you could ask me any questions, which I will try to answer. But before that, I would like to say that there is a lot that we must encompass here and that, in truth, I will always speak about the same thing, even if, on each occasion, it will seem to be something different. Thus, when you ask me a question, I will try to answer and I hope you will be satisfied with that answer. On the contrary, you are not to worry since that topic will come up again and, if that does not happen, I beg of you to repeat the question once and again until you get an answer. I expect that way, at some point, we will get to find the answer to the question you are willing to ask.

Question 1

It refers to Dr Bion's method of using the Grid.

Dr Bion: I do not believe its internal coherence to be good, but it is the best I can do, though I am sure that it is not enough. Its improvement will depend on its being used frequently enough. That's why I believe that it wouldn't stand very rigorous critical examination, although it would be able to stand some criticism, and that might help us design a more efficient Grid. I would like to do it basing ourselves on our own experience and not on somebody else's. I believe that there is nothing like one's own emotional experience of the analysis to provide the language you use with immediacy, reality, and achievement. That way we would count on a more efficient tool.

I will add some more so as to enlighten the difficulty I am referring to. I would like category "H" to remain the mathematical equation, the algebraic formulation, the algebraic transformation of a dream. The analytical work has aroused in me the strong suspicion, and it might be more than that, that the mathematical background is not, as so often it is described, the realm of the sensorial experience. For example, it is usually stated that Euclidean geometry, and projective algebraic geometry, is based on the geometry of space to which it is reduced. I would claim that statement to be correct and this Grid, in its present state, fits that situation, from the primitive statements to the most elaborate ones. I believe this is also true, but from the emotional point of view, things change. If a child could be described as a mathematician, I would suggest that the child would start off dealing with extremely complex and difficult concepts, such as infinity. From that point, he would move on to things like candy, sleep, fire, the limitless number of things which results in a kind of experience that can be condensed in the word "three". These precipitations, if so they can be called, of mathematical thought are related, or so I believe, to experiences that I would define as pre-oedipal situations. This is the assessment that there are two breasts or two parents or three people, hence, specific enumeration ranges from a point at which there already exists an infinite number that is impossible for us to count to something that can be counted and which is three. This could be suitably described as a state of "three-ness" and, for that reason, it is possible to give it a definite number. Yet, this is exactly the same thing but moving in another direction. For that reason, I also believe that in the analysis we run the risk of being mistaken if we do not take into account the direction the patient is following when he states something. Generally speaking, this is appreciated, for example, when we speak, and I hope that this does not happen very often, of a negative therapeutic reaction. I believe that this way we emphasise that there are different directions you can take as a result of the analytic experience.

Question 2

About the possibility of working with -K instead of with K and about the multi-dimensional aspect.

Dr Bion: I believe that if an analyst found it useful, he would find it very instructive to design his own Grid and, if possible, in such a way that it could be broadened to hold other areas, different kinds of patients. I think that the question of whether to use -K or K is just an example of this. The difficulty lies in the fact that we'd rather not waste time and, broadly speaking, we tend to feel discouraged thinking that we are likely wasting our time. I feel that the risk in adopting that attitude is bigger than the risk of wasting time. For example, Aristarchus developed a heliocentric theory, which disappeared with the passage of time, and it disappeared because at the time there were not good enough tools. The telescope did not exist and there was nothing that could reveal that external reality proving his theory to be right. It was not before Kepler that we managed to obtain enough information to perceive the flaws in the geocentric theory and the applicability of the heliocentric theory. By the way, this also lays out a question with regard to column 2. For example, you can say, "We will meet tomorrow at noon, or at sunrise". However, everybody knows that the sun does not rise, but it is a deception which is very useful. So, here we have a theory, with a pictorial background, a pictorial image, which belongs to category C, that we understand to be a useful deception. This is very different from the other uses of column 2, so I believe that this should also be changed. I feel it can be broadened and that nobody should feel discouraged if they design a Grid that is internally coherent, perhaps to the point that it may seem almost inapplicable. A discovery might happen at some point that may match some theory which so far has been latent.

Question 3

About the origin of the initial feeling of infinity in the child.

Dr Bion: My impression about this is that it appears as the result of a feeling of nothingness and that there exists the need to fill that emptiness.

This is also difficult to describe because this emptiness can be anything, from a specific experience to the disappearance of the breast or other situations that are much more complex and that lie beyond the child's ability to acquire. I believe that language itself intervenes here in order to fill that emptiness. This might have something to do with the possible divergence that the noises made to show that somebody was there. Susan Isaacs described a child who uttered: "U, en, u, en". After a while, it was proven that by having the child repeating, as if the mother were there saying it, "Bueno, Bueno" was the nearest the child could get to creating the illusion that the mother was present. Here we also encounter something that is a substitute for action and something that is meant to be a language of achievement, in this case, for example, the child searching for the mother. Discrimination would depend on the observations made by the analyst during the analytical session with regard to the position of the experience lived in that moment.

Question 4

A clarification regarding the difference between the language of achievement and the language as substitute for action is called for.

Dr Bion: I believe that in this case, we are to blame for the appearance of this difficulty, and by we, I mean us, psychoanalysts. In truth, only from the point of view of psychoanalysis, the question of penetrability and achievement poses such great importance, in the midst of which you trust or expect that two people having a conversation have to achieve something. This has some perplexing effects because we use words, wordings that are very familiar and that are, unfortunately, expected to have their usual meaning. However, it is not like that, as this is the question of achievement. Words can be used rightfully when speaking about Shakespeare or other writers. This penetrating quality, now, takes on a different significance both in our conversation within that intimate situation that is psychoanalysis and in the public management of the groups. Tacitus offers an excellent description of the poet when he defines him as a person capable of provoking the reaction of a tribe. He states that decisions such as war or peace depend on the intensity of the group's reactions. I feel we have here an early example of language of achievement and language as substitute for action applied to the group and which is something easier to elucidate in the management of a group rather than in this peculiar part of a group made up of two people. This in spite of the fact that I also feel that, at this point, we could say something about the internal group objects that would shed some light on the external group; the group of people.

Question 5

About the location of the material regarding this category.

Dr Bion: I believe it should be located within the emotional experience, its correspondence to one or the other category simply depends on the equation formulated by your own experience.

Question 6

About the difference between the two languages, the language of achievement and the language as substitute for action.

Dr Bion: The first step consists in practising your own ability to establish a difference. The nearer you get to that possibility you have to completely leave aside the idea that tells you that from an objective perspective there exists such a thing as a language of achievement or a language that substitutes action. What you must do is examine the material, which has been provisionally located, for example, in the category corresponding to substitute for action, in order to see which of the elements representative of a language of action are expected to be reached by *not* using the language of achievement. In truth, in order to understand what the patient aims to achieve (by the language as substitute for action), the first step is establishing a difference between the language of achievement and language as substitute for action. The next step is eliminating that difference and examining all that material that seems to belong to only one category, the category of substitute for action.

Question 7

About the initial lack of reliability of the Grid.

Dr Bion: I don't give much importance to the level of reliability which the Grid may inspire, because I do not believe it to be convenient.

Everybody has heard of philosophical doubt and they do not attribute much importance to it, but psychoanalysts use philosophical doubt as one of their most precious tools. In other words, the real matter is to doubt whatever is said. Failure occurs, to put it in Keats' words, due to the "annoying search for truth". The more tired you feel, the more irritation is released in the search for certainty, and that is the point when theories become a nuisance. That's why I believe that the day you get to trust this Grid, at least in its actual shape, it will be a really bleak day. And this can also be applied to psychoanalysis: psychoanalysts should not believe in psychoanalysis. That would be aspiring to something that not even Freud achieved. You must remain in a state in which you can tolerate the confusion of not knowing, of doubts, of uncertainty. If you are lucky, you might get to feel for some brief instants in time that an interpretation is correct, but as soon as that happens, all the situation changes and we find ourselves back in the realm of the unknown, and that is what we must get used to.

Thus, with regard to the Grid, I believe that the only suitable attitude is scepticism. The day you come to use your own Grid, you must be in a position to bear the scepticism that originates in the feeling that the work done has been worthless. This is something we must inevitably tolerate. Undoubtedly, this makes psychoanalysis an arduous task. Very few people can stand psychoanalysis, and the rest of us will, inevitably, rush into the irritating search for certainty. In this sense, I would say that when they speak about validation, scientists are way behind compared to psychoanalysis. Validation does not have anything to do with the truth. It just has to do with the emotional needs of the scientist to prove that the task carried out by him has not just been a waste of time. He might be right, and let's hope that this makes him feel better.

Question 8

About the subdivision of column 2, about the use of a statement that we know is false. Is this something metaphorical or does it have to do with negation, resistance, etc.?

Dr Bion: I believe the approach you suggest could be applied to any aspect of the Grid in its actual design, if you consider that it would be useful. I feel this is really the case in column 2. Thus, a new Grid would be created on this basis. If you take a principle like, "The sun rises", we are dealing with a formulation that to the best of a person's knowledge is true, scientifically true, religiously true, etc. Thus, the general progress of a race, or at least the mental progress, shows us that truth is limited. When we try to apply that statement, we realise that it cannot be applied in a wide way. Nevertheless, you have an application that has relevance and that makes it viable. Its usefulness is determined, so it continues to be used. But what happens is that if you start using that statement to do research into astronomical phenomena and it turns out to be useless, you hope you will be able to replace it with another principle. I don't know what that possible principle might be, but it would annoy me to have to use it to tell somebody a scientific statement—that would take me too long and it would be unintelligible for my interlocutor—instead of saying: "I will meet you tomorrow at sunrise" which constitutes a brief and quite an exact expression, not too exact, but exact enough to make a point. Thus, I think that what we are trying to find is some statement that can be used in both realms.

I understand that we obtain a gratifying experience in analysis when we make an interpretation whose aim is to formulate, in an understandable way, what has happened up to that moment, and we realise that it can be used to shed light on something that has not yet occurred. I believe that becomes something valuable, then this curious thing presents itself: the sunrise. Yet, in my opinion, this is a statement that belongs to category C because it is a pictorial image that I can visualise in different ways and that possesses a certain pervasive quality that the visual image also has. When you want to make more elaborate formulations, then your limitations become evident. I believe the entire process clearly portrays a kind of mental growth to which I would like to refer later. I think it has to do with the pervasive distance. I am not sure if it also has to do with the fact that you can see things which you cannot touch. It shows some kind of analogy to a mental extension which makes its quality penetrating. The key point here is that if we take a classic work, I guess that the ideal example would be *The Iliad* or *The Odyssey*, we will realise that it has survived for centuries. Here is a quality that has endured through time. It would be interesting to know the reason for it and then we might be able to find a similarity between that and the statement, "The sun rises". It shows a feasibility that is extremely valuable, but it lacks the general applicability to any kind of situation for which it was not designed.

Question 9

I would like to know if the two categories of language can be made equivalent to columns 2 and 6 in the Grid.

Dr Bion: I do not think so, because I believe they are not good enough and that something should be done to improve them and to adapt them to the real experience found in the analysis. Here is where flaws become apparent. If you try to use it, you will realise that it is useless in its actual state and that we need to do something to improve it. As aforementioned, I believe I have been able to use it to the sufficient degree so as to reflect on it and to change ideas as to know that it is worthless, but I have not been able to find out what else we can use to replace it. Yet, I deem that these expansions are possible and that they would be useful.

Question 10

If "O" meant reaching a reality that has to do with primary processes, with infinity, then what relation is there between this sense of the infinite and that of the baby?

Dr Bion: I would suggest that the value of symbol O, well, in truth, it lacks in meaning, but it helps us speak about it… I believe it could be considered something like a guide, and the idea of O helps us know when we are in search of truth, so to speak. I believe that, to a great extent, the same thing can be applied to truth. I believe that we never know it, and that it does not make sense to believe that one day we will know it. In some secondary and trivial aspects, I believe that it is important as a way to know when we are following the right path. As I said before, I think there is something in truth or in the search of truth that is essential for our mental balance. At the same time, the attempt to avoid the truth implies mental imbalance. As a result, I believe that this is the idea of a symbol lacking in meaning. O is the idea of something you look for, but you will never find it and that is somehow related to truth. This can be described as a verbal form to give it greater meaning. Even though I believe this is not really precise and that it is essential for the analyst's balance, just as the contrary, delusions, hallucinations, and suchlike, are as useless for mental balance as imaginary milk is for physical growth. As a result, we need some kind of symbol that does not contain much meaning to allow us to speak this way.

Question 11

About the way in which to locate in the Grid the emotional factors of the analyst.

Dr Bion: I do not believe that category G must necessarily be left empty, because it corresponds to anything that belongs to the scientific system. I believe that in category G, we should place formulations that are logically coherent and that could be described as scientific deductive systems. Beyond this, we would find the algebraic deductive system, which constitutes an even more elaborate principle. I believe that the relation between both of them is as follows: if you take the primitive principle "The sun rises", this serves a certain purpose and it has a certain durability which is evident. You also find out that it stops being a mere description of facts as it does not really belong to the realm of Definitory Hypothesis you might have taken it for. I could say: 1, 2, 3: guessing that number one would go far enough, so you would find here an infinite number of objects, but there are three and that is something. Yet, we could imagine that I would need to have the three objects here in order to count them and that I would need to set one of them aside so as to be able to say: 1, 2. And this primitive stage proves to be valuable because we find out that the formulations employed enable me to later state "3 minus 1 equals 2", without any object being there. To sum up, we have created a system that proves to be valuable because the objects do not need to be present in order to reach this conclusion.

I believe that this kind of development comprehends a wide field. One of the points about the Definitory Hypothesis is that from this moment on, development continues until it reaches the deductive scientific system. I would place this in category G if I felt the need to categorise it. I would say this is the degree of processing, the usefulness it can offer. I would position the theory of the Oedipus complex there, because it seems to offer a wide range of implementation, wider than what Freud managed to guess when he formulated it for the first time. It is always interesting to see how a statement that you have formulated ends up having an application it was not meant to have from the beginning. Poincaré also refers to this and offers a perfect description, a perfect mathematical description of the paranoid-schizoid and the depressive positions from the mathematician's point of view. When the equation appears, it finds coherence and relation where neither of them seemed to exist before. That is the value of the mathematical equation. Its application highlights a relation that did not seem to exist before. Thus, I believe that the capacity of the category is a matter of personal preference. It depends on what you feel belongs to that category, and whether it is true that it has value.

Question 12

If "O" stands for letter o or for number 0.

Dr Bion: I do not consider my personal interests to be of any importance, but finding your symbol is of the utmost importance. This symbol must be for you as expressive as possible in relation to yourself. As far as I am concerned, I believe the idea of zero to be valuable. If you can claim and you are positive that someone's existence lacks in meaning, in significance, then in my opinion, you are referring to the same thing I am. I do not harbour any doubts about the reality corresponding to O, as I am also sure it is impossible to reach. There are different ways to describe this, and I consider religious formulation to be the closest possible approach to that matter. In St John of the Cross, for example, we find an excellent description of a state that constitutes an approach to something that receives different denominations, such as Divinity. Though this term does not correspond to St John of the Cross, but to Meister Eckhart, and evolves to a point at which you can give it a name, like God. It is also pertinent to think of the Trinity in this context. This is an issue through which you discover the existence of some kind of religious mathematics that has not yet been researched. I am not referring to its meaning, but to the fact that nobody, as far as I know, has carried out any research into religious mathematical rules. With regard to numbers, in their primitive stage, no method has been designed so as to manage religious mathematical symbols in a progressive way.

The other question regarding O is the relation between K and O. To my belief, K has much to do with understanding, knowing. Basically, I do not consider it to be of great importance for the analyst because he is not interested in knowing O, but in becoming O. To be more specific, I believe this can also be applied to truth. It is impossible to know it *per se* or to try to become truth, so to speak. I believe this step constitutes an essential feature of all analytical experience: what you hope for as an analyst. Then, you become something and you trust you will be able to help your own patients find the way that will enable them to become something, that will let them be something. There lies the big difference between K and O.

To put it in other words: if we take a famous painting, let's take, for example, a famous impressionist painting by Monet, we can admire and take a picture of it and then we know K. That is, we know that the picture portrays some poppies in a field and a few houses in the distance, and we can also appreciate the paths that lead us to them. All this lacks in importance from the analytical point of view. The key point from the analytical point of view is that the experience of admiring that painting has an effect on us that makes us different from our previous selves. We will not be the same again. This is something that you cannot achieve with a photographic reproduction or anything of that kind. It is just the painting that speaks the language of achievement. If you can be within receiving longitude, in the same table of the Grid, even though it is not what we would usually describe as language, you will realise it belongs to the category of language of achievement and something will happen to you. You will become something else, something you did not used to be. It is true you can say: "Oh, yes, I know that picture, it portrays some poppies in a field." This is what any camera can do, it is what any mind, more or less cultivated or any better or worse art connoisseur, can understand. However, the next step is a completely different question: we must let the painting have an effect on us. And I believe this is the point where the analyst has reached the limits of his ability to become an artist, and it is impossible for him to establish a real distinction. In other words, to my mind, it is worth taking part in this kind of activity with the aim of reaching a point at which you can get a statement that possesses, up to a certain point, the quality an artist would to confer to it. This helps imbue it with a pervading characteristic that the patient might present and that might have an effect on him, even though I would not even dare to guess what that effect might be. I honestly do not know. But I understand this is the point where we join either the artists or the scientists, but with the aim of creating a different animal. We are neither artists nor scientists, but something completely different, even though we do not really know what it is, and I do not know if we will ever guess, at least in our times. It is a mystery, and we are just starting to learn the mystery behind it. No matter how deep our analytical experience, this is just the tip of the iceberg of that mystery.

Question 13

About the sensations, the affects, and their possible location in the Grid.

Dr Bion: I will try to face that question by using the pictorial image. The child discovers his hand. I seriously doubt this is the first thing he discovers. He might discover something like a stomach being upset which must be really complicated for him. Or, he might discover something like fear; that, at least, can be felt. I think, after a while, for most people, it might become identifiable as part of themselves. I do not really know, but it would certainly seem compatible with the kinds of things the baby experiences, such as a feeling of total anxiety, about which he cannot hold any kind of doubt. He can have no doubt of its reality, but I do not know how he deals with it, if he sees it or if it ends up being part of his personality. That requires analytical investigation. Much depends on the moment the analyst appears in a person's life, because what really matters is how the patient you are treating describes anxiety, for example as annoyance or wrath, because our experience tells us it is not so. We know that we are dealing with a mistaken noun and what the patient is experiencing is some kind of deep anxiety, so to call it. The question regarding the category where this must be located is, first of all, completely unimportant during the analysis or in tomorrow's session. It only matters now, as a means to argue about it, to enlighten your own mind, to carry out your own mental exercises, and it is really useful from this point of view.

I would even suggest that this Grid must be considered as a table game and, as analysts, we should exploit what we have discovered about children's games to give new scope to our whole formation according to trends that can be adjusted to what we know about those games. And it should be an elaborate version of a children's game. At the same time, the categorisation should be a similar blend of the leisure elements of the game and of its earnest ones, which are related to our analytical growth.

So, I would rather ask you this same question and suggest you play with it if you find anybody willing to share that game with you.

Question 14

If you, as an analyst, do not employ a tool to find primary causes or some universal truths through working with the patient, but rather help him find his own truth.

Dr Bion: I do not think we should try to reach universal truths by means of the patient. I believe that the wavelength we should reach corresponds to what you feel to be true, so as to later convey it to the patient. What he does with what you have conveyed is a completely different matter, which you do not have any control over. The only thing the analyst can do is to try to stay within the same wavelength.

I consider that what I have said here about the issue of moving from K to O is really meaningful to the analyst in this sense. It is very useful to have some knowledge of psychoanalysis, but the essential thing is to guard yourself against the moment or the moments in which you stop being a psychoanalyst to become somebody who has some knowledge of psychoanalysis. Both things are inseparable, but knowledge itself stops being knowledge of achievement to become something completely different. As a consequence, I think you can feel there are situations at work in which you feel that even though you have some knowledge of psychoanalysis, you have not yet become a psychoanalyst. Undoubtedly, it is a very long path, and I sometimes wonder if it is within our reach. You just trust that in due time, you will become a psychoanalyst, and not just somebody who has some knowledge of psychoanalysis.

Yet, I do not consider that you must try to do anything to the patient. I think he is just a sub-product, something that simply happens as a result, according to our expectations of putting the patient in touch with the truth. I find it too optimistic to think that the result of contact with the truth, as far as we can make it, will have a desirable effect on him or on other people. I would like to refer to this question at greater length, especially from the point of view of groups, within which all this can be observed more easily than in any other situation. I hope to do so eventually, because I deem it to be very important, as if I were speaking about history when I am just using it to form a pictorial image because that way I find it easier. But I do not agree with you on its being the goal of psychoanalysis. I would say that, in effect, as you point out, that is the danger of analysis, and that for that reason it is important to count on some kind of direction or to grow a state [of mind] where you have a point of reference that you do not understand and you will probably never come to understand.

FOURTH SEMINAR

Questions regarding normal development, civilised and primitive urges within a cultural container—the patient's self-definition *vis-à-vis* the analyst's definition of the problem—the survival of psychoanalysis—audience questions

To begin with, I think in general, we assume that we have a sort of starting point from which we can move, but this is not so. We have a certain idea of what is normal and of the deviations from normal, but I do not really think such a simple foundation will serve our purpose much longer. This might be useful when dealing with some very simple and quick forms of psychotherapy in so far as they are effective, but we can be certain they will not be useful if our aim is to practise psychoanalysis. Anyone who puts forward that objective should, in truth, explore it further. Much of the issue derives from our meeting with some people who at a certain point go through a critical phase in their lives. These people can take so much advantage of just one session that they are able to go ahead and never look back. They never forget the experience and they make the most of it to the point that sometimes they make us wish we could use just one therapy session.

For example, we tend to speak about disorders or about a personality disorder, but who determines these? From which vertices are these situations examined, and what leads somebody to claim that we are dealing with a personality disorder, with a neurosis, and so on?

I can explain the problem by using an imaginary figure. It is a trick that helps us abandon analysis for good and see if it is possible to obtain some vertices that shed light on some issues concerning the analysis. For instance, let's imagine a primitive human being, so primitive that he can hardly be classified as *Homo sapiens*. In such a situation, one could conceive that man to be so much like an animal. It would be usual for him to act first and, if sufficiently evolved, to think later. In such a situation, one would say that the "acting out" is normal and the thought, abnormal. "Acting out" means security, as thought can lead to death. I am not presenting this because I believe that such a situation exists or has actually existed. I honestly do not know. I am just trying to call your attention to the problem regarding direction, since when we speak about normal projective identification, in truth, we are thinking of a primitive animal, like a baby. This is an extremely complex issue upon which we need to elaborate. This is also the case for this creature and, here, I am postulating things sooner or later it is necessary to streamline, and I would suggest that is the common thing, as opposed to reasoning, which is not. From this point of view, a civilised person is not a normal person but a sophisticated person who, in truth, uses the human biological machine in a completely abnormal way, starting with the fact that we stand erect and what that implies. Thus, I think that when we are speaking of normality, it is necessary to bear in mind which direction and vertices you are doing it from.

Still on this subject, I am hoping to clarify the problem that, at least in my opinion, exists. I am saying this because I do not know if I am speaking about something that is a problem for you. There have been all kinds of developments throughout human history. All kinds of civilisations have existed and later disappeared from the face of the Earth. Yet, a question, which we have taken for granted for quite evident reasons, is that psychoanalysis constitutes the normal development of human beings and a normal activity for them, but is this so?

This implies that when a patient seeks treatment, we would like to know why he has been sent to us and why the patient has consented to come. I do not know how much you can guess in that sense, but probably enough so as to know whether you must start the treatment or not. I believe it is necessary to be a bit sceptical when a patient says, "Well, I am here because either my mother or my father has advised me to come, or because my wife says, I have to come." I do not think I would accept something like this and, quite on the contrary, I would say, "Well, but do you do everything your wife suggests? Do you always obey your parents? And what do they say? Why do you always obey them, and if you don't, why are you making an exception now?" I would like to know the answer to these questions because, in my opinion, much depends on them. If I did not do this, I would be accepting a patient who, from the beginning, would be refusing to accept any responsibility for consequences, and that is not the foundation for psychoanalysis.

I would like to give you another example: a patient claimed to suffer from neurosis, so I asked him: "Why do you think so?" He answered: "Well, I hit my head with a hammer." Another patient said, when I asked him why he had sought treatment: "I have flat feet."

The patient who had come because he had flat feet had been referred to me, as I later learned, by a doctor with excellent insight. What's more, there was also something quite evident: the man weighed about a hundred kilos. That colleague knew that the only way for the condition of the patient's feet to improve was to stop eating so much and that it was natural for the patient to have flat feet because they had to endure such weight. But he also knew that there were no great expectations of getting this patient to collaborate, unless he understood the situation better. So, it was a case in which the patient could be expected, up to a point, to take advantage of the analytical approach, which in fact he did. Even though it may sound strange, his feet improved. I guess this is the only time psychoanalysis has been used to cure flat feet.

I think pondering over this is worthwhile, because it can lead us to wonder what we understand by psychosomatic disorders. This is not a case worth pondering over, unless we do so to differentiate it from what we would consider psychosomatic and to wonder why we find it different and where the difference resides.

In the case of the second patient, it was obvious that we were dealing with a person of limited intelligence. There was no chance of applying a psychoanalytical approach because he lacked the required mental capacity to understand the nature of his disorder. It was merely a physical problem, although you can always analyse someone like this up to a certain extent, providing him with some kind of insight, but that would be a different question.

The important thing to bear in mind is that people come to us of their own volition, even if they claim just to be obeying an external suggestion. I think it is very simple to make the real situation apparent by asking things like, "Do you always do what people suggest you do?" On the contrary, "Why have you made an exception this time?" Another patient would claim feeling extremely anxious, anxious about everything. That feeling paralysed his life because everything provoked anxiety and worry in him. Hence, it could also be said that a part of this patient was opposed to another one. We do not know why and he did not know it either, but the truth is that he felt anxious. He might have had a good reason for it, but he found this situation annoying. Furthermore, even being capable of feeling anxiety annoyed him. Anyway, this is the kind of situation worth examining in detail.

Now, if you remember what I mentioned at the beginning, that imaginary creature who is developing his mind or his ability to think, we could say in that sense, "What is the situation with this person?" Does the problem arise because he is civilised and feels disgusted by his primitive urges, or does it arise because he is not civilised and he is disgusted by his civilised urges? We can consider the problem either way; however, both cases are important for the analysis, much more so if our assessment of the situation is correct.

I believe we have a certain tendency to lose sight of the fact that psychoanalysts constitute a very small minority group within a very small minority of developed states. For instance, it is essential for a culture to reach a certain point of development and for the individual to reach a certain level within the cultural development of his own civilisation before these problems become urgent. As you know, most people are opposed to psychoanalysis. They consider it being nothing but absolute nonsense. Their attitude is quite similar to that of the primitive man who acts first and thinks later. *First acting and explaining later: this is the point where rationalisation intervenes*, this is the object of his reasoning. That is, doing something and later proving how reasonable it was. We assume the most part of international politics belongs to this category.

Let's take another step forward and let's assume—what also constitutes yet one more hypothesis—that we agree with the definition of the term "psychotic". The analytical criteria, the analytical vertices would then enable us to distinguish: this is psychotic behaviour, this is not, and this is a borderline case. Therefore, we may wonder why we have adopted that specific definition, that specific point of view, and everything that can come as a consequence of this definition. Thus what is at stake for us is the question of differentiation, which is a consequence of our definitions.

But we also have this question: would it be possible to say that the patient has a definition? What he is doing at this point is complaining about some malaise and in more than one sense. I believe it could be said to depend on the points of view, on the vertices, which in reality are closely related to the principle of pleasure and pain. The patient is bothered by mental pain and that has motivated him to start the treatment. However, although just in a limited and specialised way, we must also deal with the context that patient comes from in the same way we can analyse a person who does not like it.

Does the problem end here? No, because there is another question that the analyst can at least bring up. Oddly enough, the patient brings it up this way, "Well, there is no need for us to worry about that", or "No, I am really sorry, but I do not have the time and let alone the necessary money to afford your fees", however much those fees might be. However, what the patient is stating is that he can afford a neurosis. We, as analysts, claim that he can't, but we are a minority. Most groups and societies consider the patient to be something strange, he might be nervous or a bit irritable, or something of the sort. However, they have no clue how high is the price that person has to pay for the privilege of having a neurosis. In some cases, we just find the opposite situation. The patient cannot earn his living and somebody else has to do it for him. This takes us to the economic approach to this problem; in that sense, it is a more limited terminology for the problem. I am not addressing it here psychologically but literally, in the terms of finance. Ultimately, I consider that this is what will make people aware of the price that the community has to pay, and then that community will be more willing to find some sense in the existence of psychoanalysis, or in the existence of something even better than psychoanalysis.

I don't know if this book is popular here, *Science for the Million and Mathematics for the Million* by the author Hogben, but they are excellent works. The author is a brilliant man with whom I have had the opportunity to talk on some occasions. He claims that nothing is ever done unless it is for money. Whether you agree with him or not, it is not important at this point, since it constitutes a starting point, a convenient perspective. Hogben states that when you reach that point, then something is done, mathematicians set to work, or some individuals, rumoured to be somewhat eccentric like mathematicians, acquire importance, and their work merits recognition and appraisal. But when things reach a point at which it becomes something entirely practical, then finance becomes relevant.

At a meeting, I was asked what I considered the future of analysis to be. I consider there is much truth in what Hogben says, and that the future of analysis will depend on its being able to reach a point, before it is eliminated. Here, we understand that no matter how much you hate it, you cannot do without it. That is the crucial point. Meanwhile, hatred of analysis, the simple way in which it is held responsible for all our afflictions, may prevail before psychoanalysis is sufficiently developed to become something indisputably essential within society or the social group. It is a crucial question that affects our attitude to a great extent. It is an urgent situation and we have no time to waste.

There are some individuals, very few, who have reached a point at which they feel that their mind is not an advantage but a burden. Those are the few who come to analysis. The concern lies not only in the fact that the rest do not consider this to be something especially strange or dear, but in that the society in which they live, they do not do so either. So, as a consequence, it seems very easy to afford for a big part of the society to be a disadvantage rather than an advantage. So long as this situation prevails, we can definitely expect psychoanalysis to be seen as an expensive luxury, and it will be difficult to carry out the advances in that field that would enable us to manage relatively large groups of people in a more efficient way.

I am afraid you might feel all these observations to be remote from what we have to do here. However, I think it makes sense to take these problems into consideration, because much can be said, from a scientific point of view, in defence of the possibility of adopting an approach which does not fall within the limits of scientific discipline but outside its boundaries. There is a popular puzzle in which you are to separate nine points that form a square using just four lines to do so. The simple solution to this problem might help you understand what I am trying to explain here, but the truth is that, many times, I feel the need to use an extra-analytical point of view in order to have a psychoanalytical approach. Let's re-examine the question: let's imagine we take a stance, namely, that there is a problem of mental pain and of annoyance as a result, no matter whether the patient feels responsible for it or blames others. Let's take this other stance: this one can afford an analysis or that one can afford not to have an analysis; the latter one can afford to let psychoanalysis exist or to eliminate it.

As you can see, we have reached a point at which you could say: and what does all this have to do with psychoanalysis? And the answer to that would be anal eroticism, the anal stage, and that is the way in which analytic theory arises. I believe that, in this sense, we have reached an impasse, partly due to our own unadventurous nature as analysts. This may sound harsh, but I would say that, as analysts, we devote a lot of time to learning through our own analysis and to learning about psychoanalysis. Once we have learned everything that has been written, then, in truth, we start to decline.

At this point, I also feel the need for a change in our vertices. First of all, I consider that this highlights the importance of reading only the best analytical literature. Even that is an incredibly long task, even if you limit yourself to certain authors and to some selected theories. But the crucial fact is that I do not believe that you can go on reading psychoanalytical literature all your life because, on one hand, that won't take you any further and, on the other hand, the words of any theory do not change much, no matter how long we look at them. The key point is that any analyst who has extra-analytical interest must keep it and try not to lose it. It can always help shed light on a question that has not been solved so far. In this sense, the analyst must believe in what Horace Walpole called "serendipity", a fortunate discovery by chance. What concerns us here is that Walpole referred to that good luck that allows us to bump into things which shed light on others. If you are the kind of person Walpole referred to, then you also tend to bump into things which are of the utmost importance for your main interests.

But my point is this: we tend to assume that money has its origin in a system of exchange, but again, we are dealing with a concept that belongs to the field of commerce, not from outside the commercial sphere. If we did some more research into this question, we will see that, in truth, money originally acquired its value through religion. First of all, I believe nobody has paid any attention to these facts. I deem that, first of all, it was used as a part of the religious ritual and then it came to be used to buy a wife or to pay off a crime; in other words, anything that has to do with the payment made to the tribe for the loss of one of its women, as a way of compensation, and also with the loss of one of the tribe, for example, as a result of a murder. Nobody has taken into consideration that, for example, financial management might depend on how much we consider the murder of a member of this country or of another might cost. In fact, for example, the assessment is affected by completely unconscious reasons to a greater extent than is usually admitted.

After this short excursion into the expanding universe, so to speak, using a telescope, let´s go back to the microscope. In this context, the microscope is something very complex; I believe that it is psychoanalysis itself. Psychoanalysis expresses the peculiar aim of looking into a realm which seems to be very wide, the unconscious, so wide it practically requires a model-like space itself to describe it. I do not know how mental space is measured. Anyway, we cannot do it now and it is not really important. However, if we did it, and if we could also do it while analysing our patients, we would sometimes find ourselves in a situation in which, for example, the patient couldn't afford the fees. These situations might have something to do with either his diarrhoea or his constipation. The diarrhoea and the constipation might have some relation with the primal scene, with the death of the rival, the father, the killing of the father, and the possession of the mother. To sum up, as you can see, isn't it true that we need an approach to the situation which would allow the relation between the different analytical theories to become apparent? In other words, we should begin to understand that these elements are in fact related. It is our duty as analysts to determine what kind of relation it is. We know the approach to the oedipal situation, for example, which is described by making reference to the Oedipus complex. This is applied to numerous analytical theories in which, to my mind, if you guess the myth or the appropriate theory, a connection between the elements that confirms the myth or theory becomes apparent. But now I believe that there is a situation in which the different theories should be understood as akin, and I understand we should establish these nets in connection with them.

Thus, I would like to highlight again that the amount of time we can devote to learning psychoanalysis is really limited. We need to devote as much time as possible to practising psychoanalysis, and the practice of psychoanalysis reveals that it does not stay still. For the reasons I have already mentioned, I think this is a very urgent matter.

Obviously, the difficulty here lies in the fact that our tools are really unsatisfactory. It is even surprising that analysis itself has achieved and found out so much using the framework of Freud's work. I believe it is even more incredible that the work has been continued somehow. It is important to realise how poor are our tools. Also, as regards memory, which I consider to be always based on sensory experiences, language itself has those fundamentals as it develops in contact with sensory experiences and with a specific purpose.

I believe that the real challenge is to find the way to adapt language to psychoanalysis, as language developed with a different aim and must fit a new purpose; the same could be applied to reason. Let me put it in other words: how are we to use expressions like "acting out" for a different purpose? How can we modify this process according to which we act first and then we think, and prove that one is neither guilty nor absurd, by using reason? It is an important issue because if we could sense this in a patient, we would have an idea of the direction in which he wants to use his human biological machine. In my opinion, the same could even be applied to the countries or to groups.

I would like to put it this way: to my mind, we can at least make an argument that numbers of the Euclidean geometry do not stem from—as it is commonly believed—the realm of the senses as we know it. In fact, *I understand that, for example, one of the earliest experiences of the baby is, as you probably imagine, the feeling of frustration.* In fact, you won't get very far when dealing with a psychotic patient if you do not take into account the role intolerance to frustration plays in his hatred of reality. I would also say that this can be applied to a normal person. There always exists the danger of making an interpretation simply because one has not been able to put up with frustration, because one cannot bear not to know what interpretation must be offered or what is happening. If this attitude becomes excessive, I feel the analyst tends to offer interpretations with the only aim of putting an end to his feeling of frustration, instead of doing so with the aim of continuing with the analysis.

I understand this painful feeling is, in truth, one of the first things to be measured, and we do so as follows. The baby feels that he must go from this point to that point to get, for example, the toy he wants. We can guess that is measured in feet, something quite obvious, since we use our feet for walking, or because, in general, all primitive versions of measurement are based on limbs—a fathom, for example. The crucial point is that they are later used in areas that were not their original purpose, that is, those measurements are found to be very useful in other fields. I think this is something quite frequently found in analysis. We may think we have made a very good interpretation when offered to explain something that has happened, and we realise it can also be used to explain something that has not yet happened. This represents one of the curious aspects of analysis. Namely, the patient does not necessarily learn something about his past, about the reasons that led him to seek analysis, or about what makes him anxious. On the contrary, the real value of analysis is helping the patient discover things which are useful for what has not occurred yet, for things we do not know.

Going back to this point, I suggest that, in truth, money had to do with religion and then it moved into a realm that could be described as social, namely, mating and crime, life and death, and lastly it entered the realm of commerce. As a result, I suggest that when confronted with an apparently commercial phenomenon, economists will not be able to explain it until they admit that the economic value of that mechanism of exchange is insufficient. In part, that is due to the fact that they are using an insufficient tool derived from a different sphere, and the flaws of that tool lie in its matrix. In other words, economic conflicts are the result of emotional forces which are beyond the boundaries of what we would call economy and won't be solved by a mere examination of that sphere.

Let's go back to our microscope. First of all, the description I have given is what I call a linear description. That is, one thing follows another and so on. It is very useful, but it has little to do with what I am describing, which is something very different. In reality, I am trying to describe relations that don't belong to the same class, they are very different. We would have to imagine something like a changing development field in which relations are dynamically modified in a constant way and in which the pattern of the relations changes in the same way. Anyway, up to a point, it is convenient to start off with religion, to go through the social realm, then the commercial, and so on and so forth. What matters here is the kind of interpretation we make for a patient who shows some features of a religious mania, even though this would be an extreme case. Undoubtedly, taking any opportunity provided, different interpretations would be given. In my opinion, I would not deal with that issue until its relation with that patient being a burden for society became apparent, for instance, when it becomes clear that he was complaining about his inability to make a living and also about the oedipal situation. What I mean is that the problem would not be solved without a thorough examination of the patient.

In other words, I think the only hope for the development of psychoanalysis lies in the analyst who treats patients, who can observe what is happening, and who does not offer interpretations that are internal with regard to the system, internal in relation with the *system of anal eroticism*, with the system of the primal scene, or any other system we are dealing with. There must always be an approach that implies an interpretation of anal eroticism, but which has its origins outside this system, for example in the oedipal situation. I believe, this way we would avoid explaining something from within the system we are dealing with in that moment. There is a military saying according to which the best way to defend a place is not by sitting on it, but by watching it from a nearby hill.

Question 1

About the possibility of having a four-dimensional object, including growth, and along with it the dimension of time.

Dr Bion: I do not just believe that it is possible, but I feel that we could make it possible, even though it does not yet exist. In fact, I would suggest that a lot can be said in favour of making models of this sort. After all, abstract painters just place together some pigments and we are expected to admire the outcome. I do not see why analysts should not do the same thing. I believe they can find it really relaxing and even insightful after a while. Of course, I think much depends on some kind of free association with your hands and also on your ability to play with all these things.

For example, if they built diagrams, some shapes entirely made of triangles of different proportions, they would try to see what kind of design resulted from all this. All in all, mathematicians do it, so we have those mathematical models, but we have no clear idea of their usefulness. It is worthwhile playing with this, if you feel so inclined and if you can do it, as I think it is really worth the effort.

If we think of somebody, for example, who is good at carving, I don't see why he shouldn't try to make a solid object which could be said to reveal something through its shades. In the sense of the blinding ray that focuses on the dark spot—which I previously made reference to-can also be the target of bright illumination at the same time, as there is also the idea that if you want to find something you need to be in very good light. We are dealing here with contradictions, with mere contradictory metaphors. In fact, are they two different perspectives on something that would give way to some kind of binocular vision in the field of intuition? I do not see why we should stop making such models.

Question 2

About the possibility psychoanalysis has of surviving, since it mainly deals with a time factor in a society that attacks this dimension.

Dr Bion: Of course, time is usually said to be essential for the analysis, in the same way it is of prime importance with regard to infancy. In this sense, the kind of animals that we human beings are need a maturing period, as opposed to other animals that are apparently born with a fully developed instinct. I do not believe that such a statement must be accepted without reservations. On the contrary, it has to be challenged because, as aforementioned, it is interesting to see how much time is needed in order to reach the point at which conditions are favourable. It could be stated that the more precise the analysis, the less truth we would find in the centrality of time. Obviously, we are not speaking about eliminating a large amount of time, but we know that if we can get a patient to really understand what we are saying, and if we can convey what we mean, things happen, something occurs, we might not know well what it is, but we know that it happens, and it does happen fast.

In this context, I recall the anecdote I have already mentioned. Somebody told Marshall Tate, in response to the request for a forest to be planted because wood was needed—I believe by the Navy—"Then, we had better start as soon as possible". The Marshall asked how long it would take, and they informed him he had no reason to worry as it would be at least a hundred years before any results were obtained. Tate's response was, "Then, we don't have a second to waste". As you can see, when it comes to the question of time, it depends on the view adopted by the person with regard to the issue.

But crucial here are those other vertices you have mentioned. Could you repeat them?

I would like to rephrase that question, not to answer it, but to ask it again in a different way. For example, I would suggest that we rely on the idea that man is an animal who makes tools. Yet, let's take into consideration an animal like the pterosaur which developed at a certain stage a defence system on its own backbone, something similar to a heavy armour. There is a theory, its certainty I cannot support, but which is useful for our aim here, according to which this animal became extinct because the growth of its armour was such that it became impossible for the animal to carry it. That is, it developed that tremendous armour as a way to defend itself, but at the same time, it restrained the animal. Hence, the question would be paraphrased as follows: if a man is an animal who produces tools, then his strength, his gift, just like that of this prehistoric creature, regarding the making of defence weapons, consists of enhancing his mental capability to make and use tools.

In this respect, we could ask if there exists any process whereby the capability of producing an armour and the capability of making and using tools are developed in a way that we could define as cancerous, so that man would reach such perfection in the making of tools that he would end up collapsing under them. Atomic bombs can serve as an example here. Or if his capability of making tools includes the possibility of designing a tool that could be used, like psychoanalysis itself, to control his mind. Hence, the real question is whether the ability, the essential gift, so to call it, of man suffers from an abundance of cancerous cells or if we are dealing with a more benign process.

Question 3

About the sources of Dr Bion's idea about where the relation between money and religion stems from, and its possible relation to Freud's *Totem and Taboo*.

Dr Bion: It does not stem from psychoanalysis at all. As far as I know, it is a well-known issue in works on the origins of money. In any good book on this issue, you can read about the origin of money and its early uses. Paul Eysenck is one of those authors. There is another one, whose name I cannot remember right now, who has also written on the same issue, unfortunately under the same title. Lord Keynes dealt with this issue in a much more refined way, from the perspective of someone who is familiar with psychoanalytical ideas. It is significant that when he speaks about monetary theory, he applies psychoanalytical concepts. He may not use them correctly, but at least, he has heard of them.

Question 4

I would like to know if Dr Bion considers a patient not to be analysable because he has been forced into starting the treatment, by his parents, for example.

Dr Bion: Not really, because even if the patient were three or four years old—there are different counterparts to all of this at another stage—I believe the patient must be granted the chance to guess what kind of person the analyst is. As I also understand that it is very easy to start making interpretations with the aim of, eventually, telling the child, "Well, if you want to, you can come back." I feel that if the child can feel the nature of this peculiar conversation, he might decide he *does* want to come back. This not only applies to children. I understand that the *first interview* can prove to be quite a difficult problem. I would not exclude the possibility of offering interpretations on that occasion, because of all the times when, driven by a certain notion of how to carry out an analysis, I have refrained myself from giving them; I have been afraid I have lost the patient because I have not offered him the chance to come back. Hence, I believe the answer here would be: it is convenient to give them the chance to learn what the analyst is like. Even when we cannot show them what psychoanalysis is, since they lack the required vocabulary, we are offering them the chance to come back just because they want to do it.

Question 5

Which is the real subject matter of psychoanalysis, and I would like to know if it is related to your critical stance with regard to its being a science or to its chances of survival in this society?

Dr Bion: I do not think so because, basically, analysis exists in its own right and there is no reason to carry out a psychoanalysis. You just do it or not. When there are existing reasons for it, then it is not what we usually understand as psychoanalysis. However, there is something that can be said on the matter with regard to technique. For example, we can recall the past, we can recall the development of the psychoanalytical gift in the child who understands his parents' personalities to the point at which he recognises their flaws and knows how to annoy them.

The child could be said to mature, but he keeps that gift to understand people. Depending on his own personality, he will use it in a sympathetic or warm way, in order to understand his parents' difficulties or the problems that the people he interacts with have, to make things a bit better. Or, on the contrary, he might grow up to become a person whose natural gifts might find a better use in the secret services, or questioning prisoners and developing a system for brainwashing and so on. I do not see why anybody should be forced to use psychoanalysis or the development of psychoanalysis in any particular way. We should be accepting that we are equipping people but we are not telling them what for.

I would like to express this in a different way. I would like to suggest that, as far as we are doctors, we have the target or the tendency, or the prejudice, of trying to make people's lives easier and the problem becomes a question of choice. What I am going to say might not sound really promising, but I honestly think it is true. We must take care of those states of mind which, ultimately, are prevalent in all sectors of society. For example, there are some states of mind that affect those we know as psychiatrists, there are states of mind the police take care of, and others that the secret services handle—secret services have employed prostitutes, mentally retarded people—in truth, we are working with that same material. I consider it is important to try to keep the police away from those people they employ. With regard to analysis, in the process of selection there is at least one thing we should do. The selection criteria are such that the person considered able to carry out the psychoanalysis is also a person who, from a certain perspective, might be suitable to be a patient. And the cure should not consist in making that person an analyst and giving him some new patients. From this point of view, the selection criteria become harsh and seem to be very simple. I do not always believe it to be so simple as to make the "Establishment" always aware of who is who. This way, sometimes a person's problems are solved by giving him some analytical training, making him an analyst in the sense of promoting him and letting him work with patients. If the process continues, it becomes easy, from the point of view used here, to realise that a terribly disastrous situation will not take long to occur.

What makes all this quite complex is the fact that there is some truth in the saying, "it takes a thief to catch a thief". The mistake lies in making that thief dress up as a police officer. This is the root of the matter. There must be a difference between the two situations. In one of them, the thief keeps his gift but becomes a policeman, and in the other the person remains a thief but he also learns to look like a policeman. In the same way, in analysis you really need the patient to become an analyst, and the difficulty arises when we make the mistake of enabling the patient to look like an analyst and to speak like an analyst, thanks to our jargon.

Question 6

About the location of rigid and projective transformations with regard to the paranoid-schizoid and depressive positions and the relation all this has with regression.

Dr Bion: I do not consider rigid transformation to be—I do not know how to express this—a normal development, but something which could be understood as a means of survival. What I wonder is why rigid transformation must be so rigid. It is its rigidity that is so remarkable. For example, if you happen to have—as has been my case—such a schizophrenic patient so as to have had him interned in an asylum at some point, the rigid way in which he walks, his peculiar mechanical step, will elicit your attention. That patient seems to have been able to learn to walk thanks to his wonderful talent for imitation. His ability to walk depends on him being able to remember how to walk, in contrast with most people who learn to walk in such a way that they can later forget it, and who after having learned to walk do it so without having to think about it.

Yet, without giving much importance to this theory, I believe the patient feels very different from other people, even virtually contrary to them. I do not think it is true that an ordinary baby turns schizophrenic, but that this schizophrenic baby is an abnormal baby! What happens is that to a person who is not really insightful, schizophrenic babies can seem to be very normal, since they are quiet, they behave well. Much of this would seem to be due in some cases to an early development of defensive capability which helps them know what is expected from them, and then they do it, just like walking and all the rest. Likewise, I believe that this baby learns to imitate the other children who show feelings towards the father or the mother. In other words, they display what we would commonly refer to as transference. Not knowing all this, the schizophrenic patient learns to behave in the way he thinks the other people do, and he does so by means of a rigid transformation.

In other words, imitation is a very valuable ability and, as we all know, it is part of the life of any child, for example children who pretend to be reading the newspaper. Thus, the problem lies in the fact that, on the one hand, the development of this ability for imitation constitutes a stage in the path we follow when we are learning to read, or to do any other thing, while, on the other hand, we are, in truth, dealing with a replacement for personality. In many ways, the schizophrenic person learns—and if he doesn't learn, he breaks down—to understand the environment quickly and to develop his ability to improvise a personality for whatever situation he finds himself in. As a result, when we are dealing with a schizophrenic patient, we are facing a quickly improvised personality, and his ability for improvisation can fall apart. In my opinion, if during the analysis we can, so to say, introduce this patient to his own self, and talk him into coming to terms with himself, no matter how strongly opposed he is to this idea, he will flow much more easily and the transformations that will take place will be much more projective, because the patient can project and not just imitate. We are not dealing with a rigid personality aimed at keeping others at a distance any more.

The problem with *projective transformation* lies in the fact that a patient of this kind does not really get to project his personality to the breast—since I consider this is originally what he intended—and if he does so, he feels he is confused. He does not know who he is or who the other person is. Hence, it is essential to avoid that projection and here appears the early development of imitation. It would have been better for the patient to go through the stage of projective identification in an ordinary way, so as to use it in his relation with the good mother in which his fears are detoxified, given back to him, so the child is not afraid any more. He does not learn to fear projective identification, but stops using it because it has become obsolete.

PART II

BION'S OWN ANALYTIC CASE PRESENTATION

FIFTH SEMINAR

Borderline patient with paranoid hysteria—negative therapeutic reaction—the question of transformations—role of interpretation—a victim of envy

The patient I want to speak about for a brief moment came from a family who had some knowledge of analysis, that is, one of its members was an analyst and many others had been analysed, so we can assume they knew quite a lot about analysis. Yet, the patient had a strong wish for me to treat her. Even though she had received a considerable amount of analytic treatment, she felt the other therapists had not managed her case correctly and that if she came to me, things would be much better and we would obtain the result she expected. That was all.

The patient appeared deeply troubled from the first session and she told me that, due to her situation, it was impossible for her to pay my fees, which we had arranged beforehand; but she could not do without analysis either, so we started. I must say that I did not treat this woman in the first years of my experience as an analyst, but at a time when I was already quite experienced; so, I am not talking about something I am not familiar with, at least as much as I would like you to be with regard to the analysis.

The patient mentioned two of the analysts she had been treated by and claimed that they had dealt so wrongly with her case that now she found herself in a deplorable state of mind. Undoubtedly, it was something very difficult for her. I said that, due to my analytical experience, I found what she said surprising because she was referring to two prestigious professionals, with ample experience, and I wondered if, bearing in mind what she had told me, it wouldn't be more appropriate to understand that she had already given analysis a good opportunity, and as she had gotten a poor result she should leave it aside.

I would like to remind you that the information I had did not come from the patient. She had written to me asking for an interview, but I had already heard about her previous experience from a member of her family, people who, as I have already mentioned, had considerable analytical experience. I would like to repeat that it is essential that all this information is kept at a confidential level. I do not see any way out for this difficulty, I do not see how I can refer to a case without giving people the impression that I am speaking about her; I do as much as I can to mask things so as to avoid their finding out about it, but the more this is related to real practice, the more probable it is for people to understand what I am saying as a personal remark. Thus, I consider confidentiality to be of the utmost importance.

Going back to this case, I had already concluded that the information I had been provided with was accurate and that I could trust it. I think that was my first mistake, but I would say that if I had not believed what they had told me, that would also have been the first mistake. I think that, in this regard, analysts must keep a peculiar attitude towards what they are told. This can be used to illustrate the statement that claims that while philosophers can speak about the philosophical doubt, analysts must apply it. For philosophers, it is unimportant, it is an interesting controversial issue, but this is not the case when it comes to analysts.

The patient's reaction when I suggested she might already have given analysis a very good chance and that it was ridiculous to try again bearing this in mind, became extremely violent; it included suicidal threats which seemed to be quite real. I said that I couldn't really see why she insisted that there were only two kinds of treatment for her: analysis *with me* or dying. In that moment, the patient was not paying much attention to my words and she just reiterated her intention to commit suicide if I did not accept her as a patient. It was necessary for me to say something and also to do something. What I said was: "Well, we can try." I must admit that, at this stage, that might make mistake number twelve or twenty. In a word, I find it difficult to remember something

I did with this patient that was not a mistake, or at least so it seems in hindsight.

Thus, we agreed on the fees, and the patient, who did not resemble much of what I had been told about her previously, started her analysis. For about three months, everything seemed to be a real psychoanalysis. I made interpretations, the patient reacted, I could see what her reactions meant, and what their relation with the interpretations was. Then the patient announced that she had some difficulties because she was suffering from a urinary tract infection, and this would cause problems for her to need to urinate frequently. I interpreted her comment in the sense that it was a way to make me understand, and to make me accept, that that was the explanation for her situation while, in truth, she was preparing things in such a way so that I would understand beforehand that she had an excuse to leave the room.

The patient's response was to leave the room. When she came back, she said she was really sorry but no matter how correct my interpretation was, she had an infection and she needed to leave. When the patient came back, and this is something difficult to describe, she was embarrassed and she seemed to be anxious, clearly disturbed by something; the verbal description I am offering does not really portray the situation. So, I said that undoubtedly, we didn't need to worry about the reasons she knew and we should take into consideration some other motives about which, as far as I could see, she was not aware. I said I thought, taking her attitude and the way she behaved into account, that she had felt the urge to leave in such an urgent way for psychological motives.

The first interpretation I gave her in this regard was that she went to the toilet because she wanted to know what was happening there. Her response was simply: "Rubbish" (which also means litter, waste). I interpreted then that what she meant was that in truth what happened in the toilet and what she had gone to see. This brought about a change of attitude in the patient and she became highly anxious.

However, this behaviour continued, always using the excuse of her suffering from a physical condition that made her abandon the room, behaviour that was always followed by an interpretation regarding the other possible reasons for that need. I felt it was necessary to repeat the term "as well" because I did not want to place myself in such a position that the patient might claim that she suffered from a physical condition that I was neglecting.

Yet, things continued this way, and on one occasion I saw that the patient was about to leave the room again. I drew her attention to this fact, and I said I believed she was hearing voices in that very moment, in the room. Of course, she denied it, and then I said: "Well, I believe you are perturbed, either because there are voices here that you can hear or really perturbed even if there is no voice here, because you can still hear it."

The rest of the session was characterised by a really violent emotion, consisting in denial and in asking what kind of analyst I was, how I could be such a fool so as to think that she was not in touch with reality. I answered that I had not said that the voices were not real, I had just said that she heard voices. The patient denied it and stated that the only voices she heard were hers and mine while we spoke. I replied: "Well, then, why did you say that you did not hear any voice?". The patient became furious and said I must undoubtedly feel I had been witty and clever. She added she had started her treatment for serious reasons and that she did not like an analyst who did not take his work seriously. I said she should be experienced enough so as to know that I was that kind of person indeed and the problem we were facing in that moment was why she was in that room, why she kept coming back to me when, obviously, taking into account her description, I was not the adequate type of person to be a psychoanalyst. She replied by asking me how she could face her difficulties if I did not understand the transference, if I could not understand that was exactly her opinion about me. I replied I had let myself be placed in such a situation that either I had to behave like a fool who tolerated anything or like a psychoanalyst who did not know what transference was. She could not be right in either case, and I pointed out to her again that it was quite an ordinary situation. And the most amazing thing was that, even though she guessed I had some experience, I did not say anything right, not even by chance. The patient reacted to this by standing up and threatening me with her bag.

These episodes became quite frequent, and I pointed out to her that her behaviour was making any kind of analysis impossible and, if she continued behaving that way, she would not receive any analysis and that would be the end of it. However, my words did not have any effect, something I pointed out, and I added that she continued behaving as if what I had said was utterly unimportant or insignificant. In short, she was again putting me in the position of being either a bad analyst who did not realise that what she was doing had to be subjected to interpretation or a fool willing to put up with anything.

All in all, I told her: "Here we can look into a problem, in the sense that the voices that you hear in this room—and you must bear in mind that you ended up admitting that you heard voices in this room—are in truth very angry voices engaged in a heated argument. What's more, you do not limit yourself to telling me that something like that is happening, but that, in fact, you must behave in that manner, you must make a drama out of it."

I was somewhat surprised, even though I am not referring to my analytical surprise, but to the fact that I had become so used to those stormy sessions that I was not ready for something different, when I saw that she calmed down, and I was starting to believe that my interpretation had been correct, when she told me: "You see? If you analysed me as you should, there wouldn't be any problems." I told her I thought that was her way to acknowledge that my analysis was being correct, but, at the same time, it was her way to tell me that if I had done it earlier it would have been useful.

Thus, even when my analysis was correct, which did not happen frequently, even then, I was committing an error. There was no chance of her abandoning her feelings of superiority, hostility, and contempt for me. She could always find something to criticise. These incidents continued taking place every now and then, but now they were alternated with four or five days in which I seemed to be getting the kind of reaction I described when I spoke about the first stages of the analysis, in which the patient seemed to respond to the interpretations, to return again to violence, threats, and so on. Indeed, every now and then, I felt forced, or so I believed, to tell her that those were not the conditions I considered adequate for the analysis and that I was not willing to continue in that way. Her response would be to become more violently angry than ever before, so I said: "Well, enough".

However, this is a situation in which every analyst feels vulnerable, and this patient knew it: you always feel that if you had made the correct interpretations at the right moment, this might not have happened, so a conclusion like this one indicates very ineffective analytical work. The patient knows it, and she also knows that the analyst would prefer not to finish this way. But treatment ended. The consequence was that she phoned me that night; she was truly contrite, and she begged me to restart the analysis. I just said I would think about it.

At the time, I felt quite confused by how easily promises were made, not only by the patient but also by her family; promises that were totally misleading. I just could not trust them at all. It was a very peculiar situation, which maybe occurs much more frequently than we admit.

I think that, on the one hand, the patient suspected I had been informed about her. I do not know what she expected that information to be, whether I had been lied to or told the truth, but she was positive those conversations had existed. If we want to give it a name, she undoubtedly suffered from paranoid hysteria.

I informed her I was willing to continue, but I also reiterated that what I had previously said remained in place, that is, that if she behaved that way she was not offering me the necessary conditions to carry out an analysis. In fact, we would have to interrupt the treatment.

I have previously said that it was a peculiar situation. On saying that, I have the feeling that, at the time, I must have been very young and inexperienced, although, as I have already mentioned, this happened a few years ago. I am convinced this is a situation we must consider as a real part of the analysis. The important point here is that if you can extend your ability to such a limit that even if the conditions are so bad as the ones I have described here, you do not need them to improve in order to carry out an analysis. It is a very difficult question, as it means that you expect that your technique and your analytical knowledge will improve to such a level and that they will increase in such a way so that we will be able to be even more tolerant with the patient. But the question is: how long can this process continue, and up to what point can the analyst try to establish a situation in which he can take into consideration not only the patient's limitations and difficulties but also those of her family, even though they are not in treatment?

What happened later might help shed some light on the question. We reached a point at which the patient was behaving in a more reasonable way than her family. I drew her attention to this aspect and she became furious. I pointed out her reaction to her again, and I said the only simple conclusion about this was that she felt extremely furious and angry about the idea, but in that moment she interrupted me quite abruptly and said: "I believe you should know when a patient is feeling anxious." Feeling that the patient always reacted in the same way and quite tired of her violent outbursts, I remarked that, once again, she was stating that I should be an analyst and act like a good analyst. I added that I had no obligation to be so, as I was just forced to try to act like one.

Yet, the patient remained silent, and I realised that my interpretation had been correct, but that I should say something else. And then I added: "I believe this is your way to tell me that I should be informed here about some things which are of the utmost importance for this analysis, and one of them is that you are feeling really anxious; but you cannot decide whether you have to help me in this regard or whether you must deceive me. So, you become really furious and, at the same time, you tell me I should know when a patient is anxious." From that moment on, I was able to show the patient that she was "acting" as we say, even though I did not use that term when speaking to her, a scene that in truth was being played inside herself, that is, the voices and the sounds she heard were there all the time and they belonged to an internal argument.

She replied that, in truth, her parents had been a very unhappy couple, and that there had been frequent quarrels that she witnessed. I pointed out to her that the way in which she behaved seemed to imply that those scenes had taken place at a time much earlier than she could speak. I will not go into the reasons that led me to think that, but I think my statement was correct. Once more, I was able to point out, for reasons that are of no interest here, that she was more trustworthy than me or her parents and that this made her feel anxious, because she'd rather be in the place of the patient or the child, instead of in the place of the mother or the analyst.

The patient became furious again and said that if she had improved at all, it had been in spite of my being such a terrible analyst that I could not let the patient speak about her difficulties and, quite on the contrary, I had gotten mad, speaking about putting an end to her analysis. I told her I felt she found it really difficult to put up with the fact that she owed something to the analytical interpretations and to myself as an analyst, but that, in truth, she owed part of her improvement to my insistence on keeping some kind of discipline. She replied that that was not analysis, and I responded that I had not said it was, but that I had spoken only about discipline. And then she replied: "Well, by this time, you should already know that you cannot cure a patient by just using discipline." I repeated again that I had not said anything was simple at any point. I added that, in my opinion, she found it difficult to admit that she owed something to her parents for being tolerant, in so far as she considered them to be tolerant, and also for those situations she hated, that is, when she was not allowed to do what she wanted. And *now* it was difficult for her to admit that in truth she was indebted to discipline. This was precisely the kind of thing she found most annoying, since it is hard to admit that you feel grateful for something you despise so utterly.

Well, I think I will stop here, since what I have already said poses a considerable number of problems, and I think it would be convenient for you to remark on them.

Question 1

Was it possible to modify some of the patient's traits?

Dr Bion: The patient changed considerably and I heard say, even though I cannot say how important this is, that she had improved a lot in the social sphere. That was easy to see. She dressed properly, she behaved in a different way, she walked in a different way, something that was noticeable when she left the room. I was not able to complete this analysis, although it was not due to analytical reasons, and I think I can claim that the patient had really improved, but that her hatred of me was, and still is, intense. In truth, she has never forgiven me for this analysis. I would not like to consider here her reasons for it as it would be necessary to analyse the patient to examine the problem, but there was no doubt she resented having improved, she felt utter resentment. She found the idea that she had improved intolerable, that people thought she was better, or the idea that that progress could be attributed to the analysis, unbearable.

I believe that in this specific case, it doesn't make any sense to just feel satisfied with the improvement or with the analysis. If this patient has the misfortune, and I mean it, of maintaining that improvement, then she might not complete the treatment of which she is so much in need, which would have disastrous consequences for her, as we cannot prevent her suffering a collapse. I believe that, in truth, you obtain a therapeutic effect when you insist on the need for some discipline in the analysis, but it is impossible to determine if her improvement is a consequence of it or up to what point it can be considered to be a consequence of that discipline. That's why I do not believe that it can be a permanent result, as it does not mean modifying anything at all, just teaching a patient, an intelligent animal, a new skill. That was not my impression, though, I felt it was something deeper. Thus, I am not pessimistic in this regard, although I do think that everything depends on her continuing her treatment, which is also difficult as she is kind of patient no analyst wants.

Question 2

Does the fact of a patient having had a previous analytical experience pose any particular problem?

Dr Bion: I do not think this fact can make the situation more complicated. Each patient presents special and peculiar difficulties and, inevitably, the analyst doesn't take long in finding them; what's more, I think the more effective the analysis is, the less difficult it is to face the peculiar difficulties of the individual. There is no way in which we can avoid that situation. I think we could understand this aspect if we thought about the child who is quick and intelligent enough to realise what his parents' wishes are. As you know, the child is also intelligent enough to tell his parents he had not understood what they wanted or what they had meant to say to him. After mistreating a cat, for example, the patient can say: "Ah, but you *only* just told me not to mistreat the dog." If what you say is not completely precise, the patient cannot understand, and if you do not use the exactly appropriate formula for each problem or situation, he can claim you had not said anything about it.

Yet, this patient was able to guess what her parents wanted and to use that knowledge not to do it. One other weapon she had was that she was sure an analyst could never be positive about the accuracy of his interpretations, of his criteria. In that sense, the analyst is similar to a parent who is always insecure about how correct their acts are. Yet, in his constant fight with his parents, the child always exploits that sense of guilt in his parents, knowing that the parent will probably regret what they have done if the child says: "Look what you have done." Generally speaking, they get very good results.

Likewise, along her years of analytical experience, this patient had discovered the kind of things analysts feel reluctant to do and the ones that make them feel vulnerable. The patient knew everything about what an analyst who wants to be helpful to his patient considers bad analysis. As a consequence, the patient made sure that was precisely what the analyst did and managed things so as to make the analyst feel guilty or to make him doubtful about the adequacy of his behaviour. Thus, it is not just a question of being able to make correct interpretations, etc., but of finding yourself in a situation in which you seem to have no feelings, that you are also a terrible analyst, a terrible parent. Everybody knows that people do not want to seem ruthless, it does not matter whether we are speaking of the analyst or of the parents. The key is to seem lenient and tolerant and that leads to exploitation.

Question 3

What effect did the fact that patient had been treated on two previous occasions have on Dr Bion?

Dr Bion: I think that, in truth, all analysts have patients of this kind and there is nothing special in this regard, but in this case the difference may stem from the patient's not expecting to encounter an analyst like me. She thought she was going to find a good analyst, and she had made the mistake of believing that good analysts are good people, agreeable people, and she had never ever met anybody as unpleasant as me. Yet, one of the key moments in this analysis was when I decided to tell her that she had not happened to think that I might know so much about analysis that I, myself, would be a very difficult patient, and that I assumed the same with regard to her parents, I assumed parents were born good, so to say. Poor things, they always have to behave well! What she hadn't taken into account was that, in fact, there are incompetent bad parents as well as there are bad analysts or even evil analysts. For example, when she accused me of extorting her, I remarked that it was a very important discovery, something she did not like at all. She did not really like it at all. She did not mind accusing me of extorting her, but she did not like the idea of its being true. So, I think it is very important to reach a point in which you can point out to the patient that what he is doing is making countless accusations, but believing them not to be true, and they do not take into account the possibility they might be completely right.

Question 4

In a case like this one, must the limits be set through the analyst's attitude or through interpretation?

Dr Bion: Well, I am not too concerned about this, I do not think that it has to do with me. I assume that I have said that I will try to be an analyst, and that what the patient wants is an analytical treatment. And that is all I try to do, that is my commitment. But with regard to what must be done if the patient needs discipline, etc., I really don't know. What the patient may need is a security guard. I just mean to act as an analyst, and in that sense I can claim, to a reasonable level of certainty, which conditions I need to do my work without having to worry what others may require.

I do not grant anybody the right to prevent me from carrying out the kind of work I have chosen, that is, being an analyst, or to prevent those who want to be analysed from coming to me. And I believe that, in these terms, you have the right to believe that you can carry out an effective analytical treatment under these or those conditions. But when you reach a limit, when you reach a point at which it is evident that is impossible to carry out an analytical treatment, let alone an effective one, I think it is the moment when you must set limits and decide if you want to continue or not.

I want to stress that when the situation leads me to consider that, I stop analysing the patient and, instead of paying attention to what he is saying and doing and giving him the interpretation that I have in mind in that moment and which I consider important to give him, I feel forced to consider whether this is the way I want to live my life or not. And that, in itself, constitutes an interference in the analytical situation and in the treatment of the patient. Hence, I consider it is important, as far as possible, to have a clear idea of what you are willing to put up with and also of the fact that this is not only important for yourself, for your own work, but also that there are other patients who need treatment, and you should not allow a patient to destroy your own ability to analyse that patient or another person who might be in his place. You are under an obligation to the rest of your patients.

Question 5

Does the patient described belong to the kind who, from the beginning of the analysis, identifies in the analyst a very bad object that strips her of everything?

Dr Bion: I am sure I have confirmed everything she could have said in this regard, and I did not stop pointing it out to the patient, but with her you could never be right. All in all, a critical moment in the analysis was when I pointed out to her that everything was based on the idea that it was important for me to make a good interpretation, and that she ruled out any possibility of its not being so. She simply assumed that I was not only a psychoanalyst who had the necessary resources to do that, but that I also wanted to use my analytical formation, my knowledge, my experience, to help her somehow.

So, you are asking me that question from a peculiar perspective, from a peculiar vertex, just like the patient did. And it was necessary to point out to her that she did not bear in mind the possibility of there existing another way to consider things. Yet, this was very important because she had experienced some things in her childhood she had not had time to analyse. It is natural for a child or a baby to believe that his parents are good, that they satisfy all his needs, but as adults we know that is not so, that there is no reason why parents must be good, and in this case they weren't. It was a complex situation, because the patient insisted on my being a good analyst, a good parent, in the sense I have referred to, that is, that I had the necessary training and that what I *wanted* was a willingness to help her; in truth, it was a denial of my being an extorter and who knows what else. And she was incredibly annoyed by my giving her those interpretations without denying it.

Question 6

What was the extortion and what agreement did you reach regarding your fees; how did you deal with that situation in the course of the analysis; what lay behind her hostility, was it related to her feelings of guilt due to the extortion?

Dr Bion: I explained to the patient that I had a free hour five times a week, I explained what my fees were, and I said that if she agreed to those conditions, I would be willing to treat her. The patient accepted and we started the treatment.

I believe that, in truth, her animosity concealed her feelings of guilt for the extortion, but, as usual, the difficulty lies here in expressing those underlying feelings in an explicit way. In this case, it was achieved by pointing out to her it was very important for her to feel that she was wrong—I did not tell her that she was wrong but that she felt she was—and to always stay in that situation, because she felt that if one is always wrong, it ends up proving she is right. So the main trait in all this was to continue making mistakes, not so much with regard to stating: "I am not guilty, I am not guilty, I am not guilty", but "I had more than enough reasons to behave that way when I was a child, when I was a baby, with my parents, with my other analysts, and also with you". But when you have remarked on this on several occasions, saying something like this becomes possible: "Each time you say that, it might not be very important, but if you repeat it day after day, week after week, and month after month, then it becomes necessary to consider that it is something very important and, in my opinion, its importance resides in the fact that you feel you can end up proving that white is black if you repeat it for a long time."

Question 7

Doesn't the change undergone by the patient after the first three months of the analysis lead us to believe that her attitude corresponds to that of a negative therapeutic reaction?

Dr Bion: No, I don't think so. To start with, I think it is a very unsatisfactory category. I think it is useful to count on that category when we want to get rid of our guilt or of our anxiety with regard to the patient. I do not have the slightest doubt there are things of the kind, but it is very difficult to state that we have ever encountered it in practice. *It is really extraordinary for someone experiencing a negative therapeutic reaction to go to an analyst to make it apparent*, when staying at home would prove to be much more practical.

The important thing is that, at this stage, the patient had discovered two things: she had enough information about me so as to have an idea of what I wanted and, as a consequence, to know what she wouldn't do, that is like knowing what parents want and not doing it, but she had also discovered that it was not dangerous to have feelings that corresponded to observing and listening to a man and a woman who were alone in a room. So at that stage there were three people, that is, the oedipal situation, which gave way to enormous anxiety. And we could say it is a criminal act, in the sense of having gathered enough information to be sure that the analyst is never going to do anything right, not even by chance, and it is also a situation in which she felt trusting enough to approach an unsolved and alarming issue.

Question 8

Did the patient wish for Dr Bion's death?

Dr Bion: Well, to be honest, she did as much as she could to obtain it. I think the underlying difficulty here, the one we never reached, and that's why I consider it so important for this patient to continue her analysis, resides in the fact that the situation I have described prevents any kind of loving relationship from existing. In fact, this patient is able to love, as she reveals when she tells me: "If you analysed me the right way, you would know that a patient can feel anxious". Yet, she could not cooperate, she could not tell me, for example: "Look, the problem is that I feel terribly anxious". She was doomed or condemned, so to speak, to have only one kind of relationship, something really monotonous, in which there was no room for love, for affection, for understanding but in a surreptitious way, so that nobody would notice. It was just when I managed to offer her interpretations in that sense that we were able to reach that point, even though she rejected those interpretations. Here deprivation originates in her feeling unable to love and to feel love, and, at the same time, in being able to love so much so as to feel deeply frustrated. I believe that if the patient had reached that point, she would have endured a major depression, but she would also have been enormously relieved. As things turned out, the danger lies in reaching neither that depression, nor the ability to love. The patient's behaviour may have improved, I do not assign it any or much importance, as we are speaking about a social healing, which has nothing to do with a real improvement, but with mere chance.

Question 9

That patient is acts like a hostile object to all existence; does this coincide with a concept in this regard that appears in *Transformations*?

Dr Bion: No, I don't think so, I do not think she was so sick as that.

Question 10

What importance do you assign to the change the patient experimented with after the first three months of the analysis?

Dr Bion: I do not grant it much importance. I think the patient had started to feel she knew what she had to face, but not from an analytical perspective, but just in the sense that she had enough information about me and she knew me well enough so as to believe she knew my weaknesses and to use them for her own purposes, and also that she could become relaxed sufficiently so as to suffer hallucinations. I don't think it is very important, it is something we cannot prevent from happening at some point, and I do not believe the length of time itself to be of any importance.

To be honest, I would not say she was a difficult patient, but a difficult analytical problem. Here there is no problem in making interpretations and there is no problem either with regard to analytical knowledge. It has to do more with the difficulties inherent in having to put up with this kind of behaviour. In a sense, it is more a problem of the analyst than an analytical problem.

Question 11

We are dealing here with a case of primary envy; do you consider that the patient needs an interminable analysis; are interpretations or the physical presence of the analyst as container of what the patient needs to project the effective instrument?

Dr Bion: I do not think we are dealing with a case of endless analysis, and I believe that it was really regrettable that I had to put an end to it, as I believe she was approaching a situation which would have enabled her to endure a depressive reaction, which was of the utmost importance. With regard to envy, I think it plays a role, but I do not think we are dealing with primary envy. I would suggest this term in the sense that the patient has enormous difficulty with regard to one specific aspect of envy, either her own or somebody else's. In truth, this young woman can be better considered to be a victim of envy, and I think that, basing myself on her analysis, this is the conclusion I would reach, as in truth I know nothing about her family. I am convinced she was terrified of progressing in fear of awakening feelings of envy she would not be able to bear. She managed things in such a way for interpretations to make you believe that.

PART III

HORACIO ETCHEGOYEN'S SUPERVISION WITH BION*

*This seminar was held on 31 July 1968.

SIXTH SEMINAR

The initial phase of Mr B's psychoanalytic treatment

The patient's background history—initial phase of the analysis—first dreams—the patient's internal anal universe—Bion's assessment of the patient's current state of mind—audience questions

Background information

Mr B is thirty-two years of age, Argentinian, single, and a commercial agent.

The patient consults for his inability to think and concentrate, his lack of motivation and negligence, and excessive alcohol consumption (he used to consume amphetamines), sexual problems: decreased libido and impotence (he used to masturbate habitually), and he has been depressed and sad lately; he feels anti-Semitic despite being a Jew himself, and he complains of affective anaesthesia and lack of objectivity in his opinions.

He lives with his elderly parents in a house they share with his uncle's family. He has only one sister, four years younger than him, who is married and has two children. His parents, who emigrated from Europe when the patient was six years old, managed to build up a good financial position in Argentina through their hard work and constant effort.

He does not remember much about his early years. He knows he was on the point of starvation when he was two months old and his mother ran out of milk.

He studied in Argentina, and in 1955 he entered university; but when he was about to graduate from university, he dropped out "because he was unable to concentrate, not even when he took amphetamines".

In 1960, his difficulties in his studies and in his sexual life became more pronounced. Following a psychiatrist's advice, he underwent analysis, but he gave up treatment after one year because he thought it was ineffective. He resumed his studies and passed a class in 1962, after which he left university for good.

Sometime later, and following a friend's advice, he resumed treatment with another analyst for three years. He claims this treatment brought about some changes in his behaviour and made him aware of his condition; but it did not cause significant internal change.

Due to several circumstances, at the beginning of last year he decided to continue with another analyst, and he started his treatment with me on a basis of five sessions per week.

Beginning of the analysis

During the first months, the patient kept a distant attitude and didn't try to hide his many doubts about psychoanalysis and about my suitability. He knew I had just come back from London, and he assumed he was my only patient; perhaps my first ever. (This was clearly related to his jealousy of the mother and her children.) The problems of setting alternated with the difficulties arising from the change of analyst and his desire to abandon the treatment for good. He frequently fell asleep during the sessions, especially when I interpreted his jealousy and his fear of dependency.

At the same time, he started to feel hungry when he came to the sessions, which seemed to be related with his urge to empty the breast of its milk and the penis as well. As he began to admit his need of analysis, his dreams began to express coprophilous fantasies.

Dr Bion: I'd rather interrupt the presentation at this point, if you do not mind, because I think it is important to try to imagine I am seeing the patient for the first time, instead of waiting to speak after knowing what the development of the case or knowing the ultimate result of the analysis.

First of all, I would feel uncomfortable with the patient's being accustomed to taking drugs. I would even wonder if the patient is telling the truth or not. M. Klein always considered the prognosis of a liar, the psychopathology of lying, to be poor. Yet, to my mind, it is indisputable that if we are dealing with a liar the case is serious; but, on the other hand, I would not be able to say whether the psychopathology of a liar must be classified as basically difficult to modify: I think that it is really difficult to tell when somebody is really lying, or simply misjudging a situation.

If I were interviewing the patient for the first time, this would be the kind of anxiety I would be feeling. I would feel this is a serious case and I would wonder if the patient has given up drugs, or if this is just a case of "splitting" where the patient says: "Yes, I used to take drugs", placing the action in the past, so as to not jeopardise his present situation.

The next point is with regard to the patient's doubts about the analyst. Who is he really comparing the analyst with? At first sight, he would seem to be comparing him with his previous analysts. However, I would find this suspicious; and I would wonder if I am not really suitable, just like his previous analysts or even his mother who ran out of milk. In this way, the patient seems to be saying: "I am cured, and how about you?"

These are mere impressions; but I am intentionally expressing them at this point because I think all interviews, including the first one, must be considered as first interviews. You would ask what you can do for the patient, and whether you would accept him as a patient. This is, then, what is going to be decided before the hour session finishes. That is, you must decide whether you are going to translate what is taking place in the interview into an action which says: "Well, I am taking you on as a patient". This is a basic decision because you don't really know anything about the patient and you must decide if you can do something for him or not.

At the beginning I would be cautious with this patient, and I would understand that I am facing a serious situation; although, on the other hand, I have never faced one that wasn't.

Dr Etchegoyen (*continuing the presentation of the material*): He found it difficult to pay the fees and his previous difficulties with sphincter control reappeared, especially bowel control; he often had "skid marks" in his boxers.

By mid-September 1967, a week after paying the July fees, he dreamt he was in a small restaurant and the waiter served him cat, some kind of cat stew. He felt terribly disgusted, but somebody told him he should eat it, that he would probably eat it if he thought it was hare. The stew smelled of cats' faecal matter.

After that dream, it was possible to interpret his coprophilous fantasies and relate them to his wish to feed himself in order to deny his need of analytical nutrition. Then he became distressed and he expressed clearly his thought disorder: he feels "his ideas appear without any control"; he feels that "thinking is unpleasant and awful, because it means there is something to be resolved", etc.

Dr Bion: At this point, I find it surprising that the patient expresses concern about his own suitability/adequacy. Does this mean the patient has made some progress in his analysis? Does the patient wonder if his analyst and his mother are suitable and he is the unsuitable, inadequate one? In his first session, the patient is the one who is right and all the rest the ones who are wrong. At this stage, the patient has gained some "insight". He admits there is something wrong with him, that he has some difficulties, that he is not suitable for analysis, etc. However, the analyst remains as bad as he was before and he offers him terrible food, such as the cats' faecal matter.

I am beginning to wonder if this is his way to react to jealousy or envy. The patient has admitted that there is something wrong in him, otherwise, there would be no reason for the treatment: that admission is, then, what is going to enable us to do something for him. There must be some reason for his coming to the analysis, something must be happening to him. Anyway, at this point, I would start considering whether the analysis can possibly bear this degree of envy in which the patient admits there is something wrong with him but claims, at the same time, that both the analyst and the analysis are horrible.

I am also shocked by how primitive the material is; and, bearing in mind what we have already heard, we can guess we will get to very early stages in the development of the patient.

Dr Etchegoyen: "I will read now session number 121 corresponding to Tuesday, 7 November."

After a weekend in which he went quite wild (alcohol and entertainment), even though he does not admit to it, on *Monday* he expressed fantasies of jealousy and deception.

On *Tuesday*, he arrives on time and he says he has had a hectic day, as several important orders from several trading houses have yet to be finalised, he also explains he has recently been working as a representative for the two firms he works for. He feels sad, though, because one of the big orders for Factory M did not come through, as it was given to their rivals. He has considered that Factory M makes his blood boil and he should instead devote more time to Windmill C and the ongoing orders. (He gets most of his income from Windmill C.)

P.: I had a dream last night: I was in a bar and I was served a soda. There was a fly stuck in the cork of the cap. I did not know whether to drink it or make a complaint to the waiter; in the end, I did that, I complained.

He goes on to speak about wanting to have his room tidied up and about some "associations" he had made. He had met Irma and José at a nightclub and but they ignored him. María (a new friend) had said she would contact him but she did not. This makes him think he is not very attractive. He wants to tidy his room; when he does so, he throws everything on the floor and then he starts to pick the things up and to sort them out. He goes on speaking about general matters showing great indifference.

I interpret that he seems to be determined to do in the session the same thing he has done in his room: he is throwing everything on the floor, so that I might pick it up. For example, he told me the dream but he did not give it a second thought. In my opinion, this dream is similar to the one he told me about eating cat (= faecal matter).

P.: Yes, I made that association quickly, associated it immediately. It is the same thing, but I would not be able to say why.

A.: Possibly the fly in your dream represents the faecal matter and the soda is the urine. You wish to eat your faecal matter and your urine as if they were delicacies, as we have seen in previous sessions, in order to feel independent. In this situation, however, you cannot feel independent completely because you are complaining to the waiter, who must be me.

Dr Bion: Here, again, we can appreciate some analytical progress, a development in the analysis. I think it is very important for the analyst to realise this, because such an envious patient as this one won't let you get much satisfaction from your work. And as, in truth, we need to have a clear idea of the patient's progress and what direction that progress is taking; it is essential to assess it correctly. In this context, I would offer the patient an interpretation with this aim, saying: "Well, you seem to agree with my interpretations, that they are more or less accurate, but what leads you to have these types of ideas?" In other words, it is not just psychopathology that concerns us, but also the external, real events or stimuli. I am saying this because I do not find it easy to interpret an external situation, and because very frequently the patient won't tell us exactly what is happening to him, what is conscious and known by him.

Yet, some kinds of patients, and this might be one of them, they use analysis to evade reality and to take shelter in their own psychopathology. It is at that point that you will want not just to elucidate the unconscious material, but also to analyse what is conscious, what is known by the patient. I would then say: "You must be really affected by the analysis, you must believe people who speak this way are really dirty people, people who speak about the kind of things that would be equivalent to what you would be eating, if, in truth, you ate cat's meat and faecal matter." No worse criticism of the psychoanalytical experience itself by him could be conceived, as it is not aimed at the world of reality, but at the immediate world of the analysis, with the aim of keeping the patient in this immediate reality of the analysis instead of letting him escape to a deeper world.

I agree that the patient is using analysis itself to do some acting out. I think he is behaving as if he were associating freely and instead of that he is defecating, in such a way that the analyst must pick up his excrements, he must make sense of what he, the patient, does. However, there is a trap in this, as the patient will pretend that he is the one who fixes things and makes them orderly, picking them up from the floor, when in truth, what he does is drop them on the floor and make a mess. He pretends to be healing himself and that if something goes wrong the analyst is to blame.

Dr Etchegoyen: Would this be related to the patient's coprophilous fantasies?

Dr Bion: Indeed. Putting it in more psychopathological terms, we might ask: If the breast is so bad that it feeds with faecal matter, who placed that faecal matter there?

Dr Etchegoyen: The patient now remembers a dream he had during his previous analysis.

P.: I dreamt I was in front of Hospital X and there were a group of people eating human flesh. One of these people took a putrified skull, he put some bread through it, and he ate the brain spread on the bread. It was a time when I wanted to interrupt the analysis because of money matters, and I turned to Dr Z (the psychiatrist) for advice. (He told me to continue with the analysis and that, if I could not afford it, I should do group therapy in the hospital. I told my analyst this dream, and he said I thought group therapy was "rubbish".)

A.: I think the people in your dream are the members of the therapy group, and you identify psychotherapy with eating the doctor's thoughts (= rotten brains = faecal matter), Dr Z's, the analyst's. If we put this dream together with the one of today's session and the one about eating cat, it seems to me we may think that you seem to identify eating somebody else's thoughts, discharging them as excrements, and then eating them again as if they were your own and exquisite faecal matter, with thinking.

P.: Indeed, because now my mouth is watering.

In the last part of the session, I insist on interpreting the coprophilous fantasies on the basis of his identifying confusing thoughts with (= psychotherapy = interpretation = milk = faecal matter).

In our next session, *Wednesday* 8th, he arrives feeling like crying; he is teary-eyed, he feels some kind of oppressive pressure in his chest, and he has a lump in his throat. He had a very strange fantasy in which he saw himself telling me: "X, don't leave me". Then he felt angry with the analysis because it does not cure him, and he felt like interrupting the treatment. (He is afraid he might not be able to pay me and that I would not let him continue his treatment.)

Dr Bion: I consider the interpretation offered by the analyst to be accurate. My worry would be, again, what to do with this patient, how to make him face reality. Because if analysis is so bad, why does he still come? I think that, from time to time, it is necessary to remind the patient that the fact of his attending the analysis is significant: either he likes dirt and rubbish, or he is not telling the truth when he claims that analysis is not good, that it is rubbish.

If we put together real facts (he is coming to the analysis) with what he is saying, then there would not be any explanation for wasting time and money on such an unpleasant treatment.

Regarding the patient's fear of being abandoned by his analyst, I would express it this way: "You must be feeling that if you were in my place, you would not like to have a patient like you."

It is true that the patient drinks in, breaks, and destroys the analysis. When he feels angry because he is not progressing, it is due to the fact that, no matter how good or bad the analysis is, he is such an envious patient that he takes it in this envious and destructive way, so he turns everything into faeces and then he is poisoned by them.

The patient also feels he is poisoned by what he expelled from himself: he got rid of parts of his personality he did not want, and he is afraid a correct interpretation might be like being fed his own excrements by the analyst, either through the mouth or put again into the anus, depending on the material dealt with in the session.

I think the relation has become more hostile and that is in itself an indication of the progress in the analysis, which allows for envy and rivalry to arise as soon as he becomes aware of his progress.

Obviously, this influences the future of the analytical work. I think about the kind of risks that may appear at this point. One of them is that the patient may run out of money, since without money he cannot continue his treatment, another one is that he might have a premature flight into health; he might pretend he is well enough to escape.

Dr Etchegoyen: I would like to ask you to elaborate on the patient's rivalry and envy and about the analytical work itself.

Dr Bion: I consider that to be a difficult and interesting issue. Now we have the chance to stop the analysis and reflect on this. There is an enormous difference, then, between what we can consider some kind of analytical game and what might happen tomorrow in the session between the analyst and the patient. However, one might expect to be sufficiently realistic so as to explore one's own mind and one's own possibilities in this psychoanalytical game.

One of the peculiarities of envy is that if you make an interpretation about it, you are running the risk of giving the patient the chance opportunity to say you are the envious one. For example, the patient claims that he heard himself telling you, in the course of a very strange fantasy, not to leave him. Yet, this is a surreptitious way of saying: "No matter how bad I am, don't leave me." However, the analyst mustn't take notice of this, because it did not in reality happen, it was just some kind of strange fantasy of the patient. For this reason, if the analyst continues with the analysis, it will be of his own accord, as the patient did not ask him to do it. The patient just had some kind of strange fantasy. It would be then necessary to show the patient his own vague statement is a way to beg for the analyst's indulgence.

The analyst must be willing to help him, no matter how bad the patient is; and, at the same time, the analyst should not know this.

Not only does the patient run out of money, but he is also lacking in cooperation. People don't cooperate to benefit the analyst, but with the aim of getting a better analysis, so the cooperation of the person analysed is ultimately of a selfish nature. This stage is likely to be related with the baby who wants to take things from the breast, but who doesn't want to look after it.

Thus, the analyst must be bad, he must keep feeding bad analyst food, feeding the patient horrible conversation; and, at the same time, he must be willing to treat him.

Now if the analyst does not interpret this situation, the patient will not change his behaviour; and, on the other hand, if he does, he will risk being accused by the patient of just interpreting envy because he is the envious one and not the patient. The patient is trying to make the analyst believe that he is so intelligent that his condition improves after eating his own excrements. However, I consider this interpretation must be made, and the patient must be shown the way he is not asking for help in an open way, on the contrary, he just says he has had some kind of strange fantasy; and he must be shown the way he is trying to persuade himself the analyst is jealous of such an intelligent patient, who can heal himself.

Dr Bekey: I would like to go back to the beginning of our meeting, when Dr Bion discussed the question as to whether to accept the patient or not, and I would like to know what he looks for (or finds) in the material so as to make up his mind.

Dr Bion: As a matter of principle, I do not like rejecting a patient if I have a vacancy. I consider any analyst must get used to the idea that he might be the last hope of a patient, which is difficult to tolerate. It is easier to believe that there is always somebody else with whom the patient can work. Even though you are obliged to treat people, you must also take into consideration that with our choice we might be excluding somebody who has an imperative need of analysis. Regarding this specific patient, it is difficult to say whether I would have admitted him or not, because I already know the case. However, I think I would have done it at first instance and that I would have continued with the case. At this stage of the analysis, the patient has accepted, even though he has done so in an indirect way, that the analyst is of value to him. This is of the utmost importance at this stage of the analysis. On the other hand, though, in a first session, where the patient does not know what psychoanalysis is, while now, even though this is hidden, the request for analysis is being made by someone who already knows what coming to the analyst to be analysed means, and who, even so, requests analysis.

Dr Luzuriaga: There is a question I would like to ask Dr Bion and it regards introduction to reality. I first got in touch with a technical problem while dealing with psychotic children, with whom I found myself making interpretations based on reality instead of on fantasy. For example: a boy who was pretending to open a door during a game, I interpreted that he was not almighty omnipotent and that he was trying to lead me to believe that he was, when, in truth, he was nothing but a small child who could not open the door of my office.

I would like to know where the limits are when dealing with a neurotic patient, how to understand fantasy and reality in a way that they do not nullify each other.

Dr Bion: Bearing in mind that the analysis is something so lengthy that you do not try to make it any longer with unnecessary matter. Hence, it is convenient to draw the patients' attention to what you think and they are deliberately avoiding.

The difficulty may arise of your saying one thing and the patient saying something else; but what you must make the patient realise is that through the analyst's opinion, he is saying the two things: this gives way to conflict; and the way to deny that conflict is by turning the patient against the analyst, instead of turning the patient against himself.

This process can be detected in the adult patient who understands the interpretations of his psychopathology as expressions of envy and gets rid of his awareness. At this stage, you must deal with those facts that are usually conscious in the way you deal with unconscious ones in order to make them apparent. Yet, this is not the same procedure we apply in analysis, although it has some similarities. For example, I would tell the patient that, at that point, he is feeling this or that way, and I would ask him why that is happening today instead of the following week or the previous week, or the following month, why it is happening today, and I would insist on this point and wait for an answer.

We must deal with lack of information as if it were something deeply unconscious and, as a consequence, needs to be brought to light. The peculiarity lies in the fact that it is not unconscious. The small child *knows* he cannot open the door; and, yet, we must interpret this as if it belonged to unconscious material.

This is a technical question. If you say to the patient: "you would like to be omnipotent but you know that you cannot open the door", the child can feel this as an accusation and understand that you are telling him from a pedagogical perspective: "Well, in truth, you are a very small child." We must try to find a technique for interpretation of what is real and conscious, just like we have found what this would be for the unconscious material.

We must deal with factual reality as if it had to be explained, that is, interpreted. As an example of what I mean, I would like the opportunity to interpret what I considered to be correct about the patient's difficulty in opening the door, and, at the same time, I would say something like: "I do not have to know how you got out of my office; and, if I see that you cannot open the door, I will think it was a dream. You want to make me believe that, in truth, you have left the room without any difficulty; if I believe otherwise I must have dreamt it. This way, you are claiming you know how to leave the room while knowing, at the same time, all those things you need to know to stay here speaking with me."

This does not answer your question; it is just an example. You must get used to the idea of having a technique which is nothing but a way to speak about our patients' statements.

On some occasions, patients make their claims through actions. There is an English proverb that says: "Actions speak louder than words." This is an example of a situation in which the action must be interpreted, just in the way we speak louder to a patient who has hearing problems, when he cannot open the door, the action is louder than the words, that's why he cannot hear. Then we must find a language that speaks louder than the action which speaks louder than words.

Dr Luzuriaga: I have realised that in analysis with children I tend to play less and less with them. I think it doesn't make any sense when the child just sees me play the role I have been assigned and does not listen to me when I make an interpretation. At this point, I also think actions are louder than words and, then, sometimes I do not know if I should play or not. I would like to know if this is in agreement with what you have just said.

Dr Bion: It is very important to bear in mind that the child's acquisition of speech and understanding is quite a recent acquisition for him; his ability to play and act, however, is not. Therefore the analyst is using a not-long established means to analyse the child so we must have some consideration of the inability of the child in using language. Something similar happens in the adult patient when he cannot tell us what is really happening to him, as it is based on many events that date back to the time when the adult was a child or a baby.

That's why, the analytical process in itself does not consist in speaking an ordinary language, but in speaking the language of psychoanalysis: this language allows the patient to speak up to a certain point and when that point has been reached, it allows the analyst to fill in the gap.

Sometimes the patient tells the analyst what he thinks he would not mind the analyst to interpret. Then, under some specific circumstances, the patient does not put in words what is happening to him so as to enable the analyst to complete the necessary work to make understanding possible. He is going to transform, instead, his problems into action and then he is going to act out away from the analyst's sight. The patient continues speaking through action and he does not verbalise it. One of the problems of acting out is it is made out of the analyst's sight, so one just gets a result not knowing what has brought it about.

Dr Arensburg: As appears from the aforementioned, the patient seems to be hiding in language what he later shows in a different way, in acts that speak louder than words. I would like to ask Dr Bion, then, if acting out does not reappear again and becomes apparent to the analyst in these unspoken acts that are carried out during the session. That is, I would like to know if a repetition of the acting out might occur during the session, in a form of acting which would, however, keep the characteristics of an acting out.

Dr Bion: This is a very important aspect and that's why I want to insist on the acting out that takes place out of the analyst's sight. When we make an interpretation in the analysis, we expect the patient to bring the conflict to the session, just as we would expect a child to go on playing. The patient's progress lies within the ability of the analyst, who can, at least, ascertain his actions. On the contrary, if the patient acts instead of speaking, he will be repeating this same pattern in his life.

SEVENTH SEMINAR

Mr B's psychoanalytic treatment in the following year
The problem of excessive projective identification—further dream analysis—the difference between the patient's own model of mind *vis-à-vis* the analyst's model of the patient's mind—Mr B's difficulties in paying for his analysis—audience questions

Dr Etchegoyen (*reading*):

Development

In the months that follow, you could see a change in the patient's attitude about the analysis that at times looked like it sparked his interest. He attended with increased regularity, and he was worried about his difficulties in cooperating while he accepted more and more that he had a certain separation anxiety.

Week of 10 to 14 June 1968

In this week, when he was almost caught up with paying all of his fees, certain themes reappeared from old material. During the session of

Monday the 10th, he said he was pretty confused over the weekend. He ate and drank excessively and felt a certain type of relief when it was about to be Monday. Sunday night, he dreamt that he was in a bathroom and wanted to wipe or clean himself, but he couldn't because there was dirty water coming out of the faucet at the same time that he kept dirtying himself continuously. "It came out of my rear-end", he adds, "a certain type of liquid shit, drop by drop, that dirtied me constantly". He also dreamt that he was with Roberto and his cousin Luisa. Roberto explained that he had this woman touch his penis while he was fully clothed; and he was excited about it. He was able to control his own excitement, so that he was able to avoid having an orgasm. The patient congratulated him (Roberto) for being able to control himself.

Tuesday the 11th, he started by apologising for not being able to pay me in full. His cheque that he gets for his work at windmill "C" is ready, however there were no funds available for him to cash it—even though that was a rare occurrence in that business. Nevertheless, he asked them for an advance, so that he could pay me tomorrow. Then he noticed that he asked for a lesser amount of money than for what he owed me; then he said he has difficulties in paying me, but at the bottom, he thinks that I can always wait to be paid. Then he starts telling a dream: I am driving my car on a wet street, and the brakes are failing. (This seems to be related to his acting out and a loss of control over the weekend and his fear of losing his own bodily products = money = faeces.) Then he recalls another dream: he is in a small port town, unknown to him. He has gone there either because of work or because he wanted to visit the place. It is night time and he decides to go to places where he can have fun (even though he thinks that it is unlikely to be available in this type of place—that is, women to have fun with). Then he arrives at this house, a type of country house; it has a backyard with many trees, where he sees that there are women and men who are partying. And Roberto shows up with two prostitutes, who are side by side with him.

He associates to the type of life Roberto has. Lately, he has started to understand that R has an unbridled life. He admits that he used to do the same, but he has never realised how in excess it is, as if he is over-medicating himself. And then, he remembers that R used to be part of a psychotherapy group; and that he ended it by going to bed with a couple of members of the group—and even with the therapist.

I interpreted his wish to change the analysis into a game with prostitutes. The two prostitutes who appear with R are his two analysts—the one before and his current analyst. And at a deeper analytic level, two breasts that are degraded. And then he admits that the analysis does not have any *sentimental* emotional meaning, but is a mere financial or commercial transaction.

Dr Bion: A very important point is to ask why separation anxiety appears so intensely. Do you have any thoughts about this?

Dr Etchegoyen: The patient has been in analysis for over a year and, during this time, it was possible for him to understand his need and dependency for the analysis and the analyst. This material repeats itself in two circumstances, even though it wasn't specifically selected for that purpose. However, as an example, in the first case, the patient did not have any awareness that the weekend had caused him to feel confused and to drink excessively. However, in this case, he had a sufficient awareness of that.

Dr Bion: The most important thing about this is when the patient has no reaction to the interruptions. Obviously, the most common interruption is the weekend or its equivalent. I think that patients get used to the interruption at the end of the sessions—and they take it for granted. When the weekend arrives, the interruption is longer, and you hope that it is going to stimulate something.

Then it is important to show to the patient that, during the weekend, he feels little contact with people in such a way that he is not even aware whether his analyst is present or absent. Nevertheless, on the other hand, the reaction due to the weekend interruption shows that he is aware of the presence of the analyst—he notices his absence in that way. All of this refers to looking at this superficially. So the question to ask, nevertheless, is which way does the patient react to the end of the analysis—even though it is a reaction to the stimulus of a temporary termination.

Continuing to talk about the dream, I would say that a part of the dream again (at a superficial level) expresses his feelings of inadequacy: the patient wants to clean himself, but doesn't know how to do it. I think it is legitimate to assume that the patient has fears of the termination of the analysis—that there won't be anyone else to clean him. But he feels the loss of the analyst like a baby; he will have to be cleaned. He will feel the type of loss that babies feel because babies do need to be cleaned by someone else. I wonder why this happens because if we consider the facts in reality, it is an argument about theory when the analyst interprets, he is offering a theory he has about the patient. When the patient free associates, it is the same: he expresses in a different way the theory that, ultimately, the patient has about himself.

For these reasons, one would have to ask why the patient would feel that he is not able to be without the analyst, and why would he consider the analytic process to be a cleansing one. To follow this line of thinking, I would say that the patient has the impression that he is coming to the analysis to get rid of his symptoms. And when he gets rid of them, he goes back to a very primitive state of mental life, in which the first experience of getting rid of something is defecation.

Nevertheless, another of his peculiarities is that it feels obvious that he doesn't really get rid of his symptoms, and in this he expresses, again in a rather primitive way, the child's anxiety that he discovers by defecating, one he hasn't really finished so he feels that whatever was defecated comes to him again. And this is why he has to defecate again and again.

There is, then, the feeling of persecution in all of this. The patient feels that coming to analysis recapitulates very early experiences, such as having a bowel movement, and he feels that he is never able to get rid of anything because everything returns again.

I would like you to continue the discussion because I feel it is very important to be able to elaborate two themes: the first is why that theory of the patient exists; and the second is to which of the existing analytic theories does it approximate?

What is fundamental in any analysis is to have an alignment between what you feel is happening with some existing theory in that regard. It is for these reasons that I think it is very important to have some sort of contact with the patient, which permits us to be aware of what is going on. Once you know this, then it is easier to know what the patient expresses and what is his theory. One ought also to take into consideration the combination of these two things, that is, the two theories.

The patient doesn't feel capable of self-analysing or being without the analyst, nor getting rid of his symptoms. It is like the faecal material: you always have it, or the patient always has it. Not even after defecating can you get rid of it, and this dirties the patient, which suggests that this refers to evoking early experiences that are still valid or ongoing for the patient.

Dr Etchegoyen: I think that the patient has also put faeces in his mother's breast, like we see on the faucet that appears in the dream.

Dr Bion: Yes, in fact, that is the case. It appears that he is aware of the sexual stimulation during the cleaning process. Roberto explains in the dream that he had this woman touch his penis over his pants. Well, in fact, if he gets dirty, he has to be cleaned again, even when we may not know what kind of stimulation he might get in that. Of course, Roberto is a part of himself in the dream.

The idea of pollution suggests again that this is about something that is bad or dirty, of something that dirties, or dirties one, which takes us again to the idea of faecal material. The patient thinks that this is exactly what the dream says. Even adult sexuality is utilised by the patient to dirty something or somebody, as if he had something dirty inside of him.

Dr X: Dr Bion points out that, probably, there is certain evidence in the clinical material of an infantile situation related to the personal experience of the patient. I would like to ask if Dr Bion, when he is positive about the existence of the evidence, interprets not in today's session but in relation to the past with a certain historical reference.

Dr Bion: I would like to say that in a case like this, there is a certain reminiscence of the past. I point out the fantasy of the patient and its possible reference to the past.

Dr Etchegoyen: Another important fact about this material is that the patient is not only feeling separation anxiety about the weekend, but also the anxiety about having to pay his fees, which for him has a very special significance. I would like then to have Dr Bion speak about this.

Dr Bion: I would like all of you very much to discuss this matter, because I think that the analyst gets into the habit of making interpretations either because you have experienced your own analyst making interpretations to you in your own analysis or maybe because you have read about them. This is obviously very different than making an interpretation because you have heard it during the session.

I am sure that there is a big difference in the impact and penetrative quality of the interpretation if the patient feels that it is personal to him, with which he would be in agreement—or not, depending on the situation, and this is something very different from when the interpretation refers to a book, to psychoanalysis, or to Freud.

I think, before you read a lot of psychoanalytic literature, it is fundamental that you develop your own collection of analytic themes, subjects, and then, when you think you have found a good fundamental description of anal-erotism, for example, then you work with it. It is of fundamental importance that you deal with these subjects as if they were completely new—never discovered before in such a way that you will discover the theory and the interpretation instead of these interpretations being transformed into something that is imposed on you.

I talk about this because it is related to an arc of interest for psychoanalysis. When the patient returns every Monday to get/receive more analysis, the analysis is also inadequate. When the patient interrupts the analysis on Friday, the patient is inadequate. In the first place, I believe that the patient is much more affected (impacted) by the analytic conversation than what he admits or says. I think that the analytic conversation is clean because the name "psychoanalysis" makes it respectable.

In other circumstances, if two people are talking about penises, breasts, and similar things, they are having a "dirty" (or sexual) conversation. I believe then the patient thinks that the analysis is going to be as helpful as when the child is playing sexual games with another child.

It takes a long time to understand what he learned in the sexual games can be useful later on. Then, I believe that the feeling of despair and helplessness is related to the idea of having the analysis. Because the patient plays with his penis like a faucet—he can't really feed himself with it because that milk is very dirty (i.e., milk as urine). And if ever he tried to eat his own faecal material, his corporeal bodily products, he will find out anew that while this won't poison him, it also won't nourish him.

In many different ways, all of this expresses his anxiety about hopelessness and helplessness. It is not worth it to go to the analyst, nor to himself, or even to other people. Of course, I believe it isn't necessary to clarify that in this dream, as in any others, that the names of all the different people who appear have any particular meaning. But in this case, we are talking about his own dream—and not that of Roberto or Luisa talking with him. In reality, it is he talking with himself through all these different characters. He congratulates himself for his self-control, or the control over his impulses—which is inadequate. The analysis is in itself unpleasant and dirty, and other treatments, such as self-control, are bad.

In the description of the weekend, something similar occurs. He has a bit more curiosity, he goes to a night-club and eats and drinks in excess. Here a new element appears—which is his voraciousness. I believe it very important to analyse the voraciousness, but I also have to say that we don't know what its cause is because, if the patient is not getting better, all he can do is want more and more—even though he does not know what it is that he wants more and more of. This is very important because babies have similar situations. For example, let's assume that the mother is not very loving and baby is withdrawn without feeling fully satisfied. It is impossible for the baby to know why he is so withdrawn, he is just wanting more and more milk. However, this is not more and more cure. It is important to point out the difference between having more and more analysis and more and more dirty conversations. The psychoanalyst is not going to give the breast, and even if he's offered it, it would not change the situation because a breast no longer has the meaning that it would have had in an appropriate time and place. (This is also one of the defects of psychoanalysis, that is to say, we can consider that the analysis can be effective for the time between the psychoanalyst and the present state of the patient, but it cannot cure what has happened before. Whatever happened before continues to persist within the patient.)

Another element that appears is voraciousness—more analysis, more milk, more self-analysis. This is something similar to a mental masturbation, but it is not a cure. It is only more and more voraciousness because he can't get what he wants—all he can do is to continue being more voracious. I believe we have discussed this matter sufficiently to show the issue that the patient is voracious. If fact, his associations are voracious because he formulates them in such a way that it is very difficult to satisfy them. If you take up the point of view that his associations help the analyst, so that the analyst will give him more and more analysis—and in this way, satisfy his voraciousness. The analyst can offer him good interpretations, but he can't resolve what he didn't get in the past.

Generally speaking, how does he take care of the fees?

Dr Etchegoyen: He pays, but he is always behind. On this occasion, he was just behind a little bit, but he was very worried about it—even though I wasn't asking him for anything.

Dr Bion: Do you ask for the money, or do you give a statement to the patient?

Dr Etchegoyen: I don't give a statement. I wait for him to pay me.

Dr Bion: But it was already arranged beforehand what the patient would pay?

Dr Etchegoyen: Yes, he knows; but he has to figure out the amount and he has to pay between the 1st and the 10th of the month.

Dr Bion: Then, the patient knows how much he owes you and is able to figure out how many sessions he has had. Habitually, you don't ask him for the money—and you didn't do it this particular time (that session) even though you know the patient will pay within the agreed time (between the 1st and the 10th of the new month). What did you mean when you said that the patient was going to receive a salary?

Dr Etchegoyen: The patient has an income for the work he does at the windmill.

Dr Bion: It seems like an ambiguous phrase. Is it up to him to get the money to pay the analyst? Or should the analyst pay the patient? Do you understand this ambiguity?

Dr Etchegoyen: Yes, I do.

Dr Bion: You should receive your compensation from Windmill "C". What does this mean? Consciously, I am not talking the unconscious meaning.

Dr Etchegoyen: The patient was waiting to be paid at el Molino in those days.

Dr Bion: What other meaning could this have? Could it be some sort of word game?

Dr Lururiaga: *Which* phrase?

Dr Bion: In el Molino "C".

Dr Lururiaga: No, it cannot be. The material is not textual. It doesn't have anything to do with el Molino. We switched it for reasons of confidentiality.

Dr Bion: Do you not remember the exact words?

Dr Etchegoyen: I would rather not explain this, and I think it is unimportant.

Dr Bion: I think I was probably misguided by the printed materials and my own associations to it. What happens is that we are accustomed to having double meanings, especially when it relates to money. One might prefer to ignore if in reality that double meaning may—or may not—exist. But again, we can see the inadequacy; he should have paid the analyst before; and he should also have been paid before (for work at el Molino).

Anyways, I suspect that in this, we can see what I have already mentioned before. In a certain way, what begins to appear in this psychoanalysis, including if the analyst was paying the patient, he would not be able to cure him. (In a similar way, if the patient pays the analyst, he doesn't pay him what (everything that) he would like to pay.) Whether this is hate or love, the patient is trying to express through the act of paying (or whatever he wants to express by paying). In conclusion, because the patient does not pay the analyst, one could say from this perspective, that his behaviour is inadequate; and from another perspective, this patient is financially constipated.

Dr Etchegoyen: In fact, the patient did lose faecal material through his anus.

Dr Bion: Yes, but in the way he does this, the fees he is paying are too small.

He drains/loses faecal material permanently, in such a way that he loses all his money—and in reality, he doesn't pay the analyst because these are the only small drops he has given. The patient is also saying that el Molino is inadequate. Here you ask: what does this mean?

Under these circumstances, it is easy to fall into a trap. The psychoanalyst is persecuted by the feeling that he doesn't know how to do analysis, or that he doesn't have sufficient interpretations. I think in reality that the feeling of the analyst's inadequacy doesn't have much meaning. Superficially, we might think this way—we don't have the patient here, but we do have the analyst, and we could continue asking him questions. I don't literally mean to ask questions, but to rather wait and listen to see what the problem is. I will say it in the following way: when we ask about anal erotism, for example, I think that the tendency is to ask on the basis of a theory. But if we do this, I include here, even in this supervision, a suspicion we start interfering with figuring out what is going on in the analysis. I think that if you do this, you will interfere with paying attention to the patient. The time that we have with the patient is very short. We should remember that even if the patient comes five or six times a week, it is still a few hours of his total time. It is for this reason that we must not lose anything of the session, within his capabilities. I think that the analyst should be voracious in this aspect. With all his senses awake, he should do his best.

There is an important point—and it could be that the patient is inadequate, but he has an easy remedy for that—simply satisfying the analyst by getting the money from his mother, like el Molino. In this way, the patient doesn't have *any* direct contact with the analyst. He doesn't pay him directly, neither does he compensate him by getting better. What the patient does is obtain money, pass along to the analyst, and remain outside. The reason I am asking these questions is so that you can think about these questions as well. I think that psychoanalytic "training" ought to be treated like a game, that it is seems both serious and fun like a game.

We recognise the problems that it presents with those patients who have inhibitions in playing. We consider this a very serious symptom. The child who cannot play is always a very disturbed patient. Nevertheless, one can repeat similar mistakes in analysis. Our psychoanalytic training is neither serious nor fun—and it should be both. I don't know how the training was for you, but for me, I never experienced a more difficult and terrible time in my life. I went to conferences and seminars that occurred in small, hot rooms filled with smoke, with an analyst who was exhausted (as the students were). It wasn't anybody's fault, it was simply that analysis had to be learned and taught in the time we had free.

Dr Bion: I would like now to call attention to this point, but from a different angle. The patient is enacting the financial situation with the analyst. He transforms himself into a third person who has no responsibility to pay. At the Molino, he can always say: "I am sorry, but my analyst leaves me so depleted of money that you are going to have to pay me." And in the same way, he can say that to the analyst as well: "I am sorry, but I can't pay you, as the firm is not paying me." In none of these cases does the patient have anything to do with money. In certain forms, this typifies a certain social problem. I think that if one feels this way, he then justifies difficulties for the terrible costs of the analysis.

There are patients who are, many times over, a heavy financial load for the analyst to carry—as well as for themselves, for their families, and for the state. So, the problem of paying is really a consideration for the analysis, and it affects the patient as well as the analyst. Nevertheless, there is also a broader consideration about this situation. If it would be possible that this economic burden for the community could transform itself in a certain financial achievement, something important has been done.

Another interesting point: the father and the mother but not the patient are the ones who have a relationship in which they mutually defecate and urinate on each other. Nevertheless, the fact that the patient dreams about where he dirties himself constitutes an important remembrance. It doesn't relate here to the mother and father and how they cover everything with faecal material, but how he himself does it. This in spite of how the patient keeps talking about the mill and the analyst, father and mother.

There is also another important aspect, which is the fact that the patient barely speaks with the analyst, and does not maintain the dirty conversation with the analyst, but he speaks only about "respectable" psychoanalysis. Who then is maintaining this dirty conversation? Because there are in this moment three people in the room: the analyst, the patient, and another part of the patient (another him).

Dr Etchegoyen: I would like to ask Dr Bion about the relationship between the faecal material and the thinking process, about coprophilic fantasies, in this patient. I would also like to know what he thinks of the thought disorder in this patient, because he consulted the analyst, among other things, because he couldn't think and he found it very painful.

Dr Bion: In this case, again, I would insist—I would not try to think about the thought disorder or other psychoanalytic theories about the patient. I would think that the analyst cannot speak with the patient—and vice versa. This is what apparently *is* happening; I understand by way of the analyst that it is true.

Therefore, even though I am not present at the session, I am going to assume that the same type of situation occurs in the patient. I would think, as we have seen until now in terms of the container and contained. That is to say, that what the patient wants to transmit to the analyst does not go anywhere, it is unimportant, superficial, and the same is true of the analyst with respect to the patient.

Srta Evelson: The patient consulted because he couldn't think, or because he wasn't capable of thinking. I would like to know if Dr Bion thinks that this is what is happening in the session, in other words, the mutual impossibility of the analyst and the patient putting their own contents into the other, which is related to the difficulty that the patient has in thinking.

Dr Bion: I don't have any doubts about it. In the moment that the patient says this, he feels very adult and sophisticated, very identified with the analyst and with other adult people. In a way in reality you would not know what this means, then you would wait for the meaning to appear at any moment. What the analyst should be capable of seeing is what is happening, which is the distortion in the relationship between the patient and himself.

I think that one can feel that, in one way or another, there is a transformation. What is important here is to decide if in this dialogue what you are listening to is *only* a dirty conversation—or only a theory, in a way that everything related to sex, etc., escapes. Or, maybe that the conversation is what was listened to but not the method that was used. Is this the analyst who is trying to put dirty noises and farts (the breath when you speak) inside the patient? And vice versa, the patient.

That is to say, it turns out that the patient doesn't hear the dirty conversation or, if he hears it, he doesn't pay any attention to the analyst putting farts inside of him. In this manner, the patient tries to not think that he is the one who is putting farts into the analyst. As long as the patient is unaware of this, he feels hungry: an important part of the conversation is excluded, and is totally missing.

Dr X: Does this mean that the patient is negating/denying his fantasies of dirtying the analyst?

Dr Bion: The patient is both denying and expressing his fantasies. Because even when his fantasies do not show up in the conversation, when he goes to sleep and drops his guard, the fantasy shows up in his dream.

PART IV

BION'S FURTHER SUPERVISORY WORK WITH OTHER ARGENTINIAN ANALYSTS

EIGHTH SEMINAR

An "in-the-moment" presentation of an adult analysand, all with no orienting background history—audience questions

When Dr Bion was asked how he'd rather have the material presented to him, he says that the clinical material could be read straight away and that when he needs some clarification he will ask. So the session commences.

Clinical material 1

Patient: This is the book I spoke to you about. (He gives me a thick book which I open. I feel surprised to find that it contains only figures, numbers. As he lies down, I leave the book on my desk.)

Analyst: With this book, you are showing me all those things you would be missing if you became an analyst; you feel that you are gaining important things but you are also losing all this, everything this book contains: the physical aspect, the body. I have felt you were giving me something in the form of a sacrifice, as if it were some kind of holocaust.

Patient: Yes, there was also something in Z (his previous group therapist) which I found hard to come to terms with. Not so much with you, but I found it really difficult to admit that Z was a doctor and had studied the same subjects I had. I think and I know that you also studied pathological anatomy and that you worked hard in physiology just like I did, but I find it hard to accept. I think you come from some other place, from another school, from another faculty. Once I told him that I would need him to wear his white coat, for me to accept that he was a doctor.

Supervision

Dr Bion: Why did the book surprise you?

Analyst: Because I only found figures, columns of figures, I had thought it would be a text. I was surprised because he had often spoken to me about that book and about another one by Finkelstein, a paediatrician devoted to theoretical studies, and he believed the book he brought me to summarise all paediatrics. He said if he ever became an analyst, he would keep those two books, the rest of them he would sell or give away.

Dr Bion: What comes to my mind is this: why has the patient given that book to the analyst? He could have done it before speaking about it. Why has he stopped speaking, giving him the book in exchange? The patient wanted the analyst to feel surprised, perhaps shocked. Can we know enough about the language the patient uses so as to know what shock means for him? What I know is that he has given the analyst something that is precious for him.

Analyst: In that moment, I thought of some kind of ironic remark, like saying: do you know all this by heart? But I did not tell him anything.

Dr Bion: I think we must bear in mind the fact that in an analytical situation the patient does not speak in a sequenced way, and neither does the analyst. Somehow, it is an ordinary conversation, but from a different perspective, it is not: in our daily lives, you do not make interpretations. This patient could have entered the room and spoken about the book as he had previously done or he could have said: "I had a dream about the book". However, he says instead, "Here is the book". In other words, I think he has modified his language.

The shock of the analyst is interesting because, according to the patient, he had to be shocked. I guess the analyst's reaction is correct, that this was what was expected.

This makes us wonder: what is the meaning of the book? Is it that it contains everything the analyst knows, or is it the fact that its pages are covered in signs? Must the analyst react as a child would at opening a book and finding signs? Supposing a child is being read to and he looks at the book to find nothing but printed signs. There is no tale; just black marks. Is this a way to make the analyst feel a particular way? My question would be: what does this language mean?

Analyst: Would you formulate this as an interpretation? What would you do with the book?

Dr Bion: I don't know. Here I have the luxury to think, with the patient I would not be able to. There is an enormous difference between what we are doing here and what we do in the analytical session, because there you must think or say something, here I just want to share the surprise felt by the analyst. I think I would have browsed the book and its figures and, at the same time, I would have expected him to tell me something. I would have said: "I can see many figures here; can you elaborate on this?" This is what I think of now.

Analyst: I interpreted the feeling he was giving me something he did not really want to give me completely, as if it were some kind of sacrifice.

Dr Bion: I do not know what makes you say that, but the analyst has lived a long history with the patient before this. The analyst knows the patient, and I do not know anything about the case.

Clinical material 2

Analyst: You do not know if you can identify with me, if I am going to offer an appropriate image for you to do it. You tell me that I am more a father-doctor-analyst than Z for you, but, all in all, you find it difficult to accept that because you do not know if you are going to attain a good identification with me. You describe me as made of sterner stuff, which means that you will never be like me, you will never get to be what I am for you in your fantasy.

Patient: You know what? From the first day I saw your medical diploma. I have never seen Z's, he does not have it in his office. These are small things, but I felt him more indifferent to the medical profession, now there exists a different kind of relation within me. In the group, at the beginning, I felt ignored; however, in the study group we have in the hospital with P, there are residents, doctors, several psychologists, and me. I don't know, yesterday it might have been because of some kind of misunderstanding, but P did not come. Last Wednesday, we had to call off the meeting we were to have with him, and they said they were going to let him know to attend this Wednesday, but they did not.

I don't know, then all of us met and we went on chatting, and then I realised it. The psychologist remarked on it as well; she mentioned that she had noticed a change in my attitude. I really felt it to be that way, we were speaking about issues I felt comfortable with and which I understood, and I was even able to shed light on and to explain things to the psychologists and to the other residents. As I was explaining things to them, I realised that as I was explaining them they became clear to me. Some months ago, even before I started my analysis here, at the end of last year, I really felt out of place, a bit shy or inhibited in that group, I would listen and whatever they said I felt to be incomprehensible and extraordinary from my point of view.

Analyst: In your story, you describe yourself as seeing things more clearly and explaining them to the rest of the group; however, your attitude today since we started the session has been that of covering your eyes as if a part of you wanted to see things and, what's more, you seem to see them, and, on the other hand, that makes you quite anxious and you cover your eyes so as not to see them.

Supervision

Dr Bion: What was he doing?

Analyst: He was lying down covering his eyes with his hand.

Dr Bion: Was the tape recorder there?

Analyst: Behind the couch I have a bookshelf. The recorder is always there, but I do not usually record my patients without previously discussing it with them. However, on this occasion, I decided not to tell him.

Dr Bion: And do you think he did not know it?

Analyst: If he had wanted to, he would have been able to see the recorder.

Dr Bion: Would he have been able to see if it was on?

Analyst: That is more improbable.

Dr Bion: He could have seen it or not. He could have thought it was on or not.

Analyst: Indeed.

Clinical material 3

Analyst: The dangerous aspect of his fantasy of becoming an analyst is that even though he really longs for it, it is also something forbidden. On the one hand, he tells me he understands the analytical material much better and can even teach it, but on the other hand, he does not want to see it because he is afraid of doing something wrong.

Dr Bion: Do you think he thought he could get to a point where he could see and he did not want to?

Analyst: To my mind, he was afraid to admit he would have to undergo a long and deep analysis and that he would suffer as a result. At some point, we saw that before being able to decide whether he wanted to be an analyst or not, he would have to comply with another procedure, he agreed to be analysed, but in such "light" a way as possible, so as to become an analyst.

Dr Bion: Could you please explain why you made that interpretation?

Amalyst: In his record, I include a dream which was really traumatic. We spent several sessions analysing it, and he was really moved by all the things that stemmed from it; it was the first time we understood he was going to suffer during the analysis.

Dr Bion: What made you think in that session that the dream was important?

Analyst: I felt I was experiencing the entire atmosphere of the dream, which we had been speaking about in recent sessions and which we followed as if it were just one session interrupted several times.

Dr Bion: I think this sheds light on this and it is highly significant, as I guess the patient is afraid of what he will see or hear in this session. I think the patient is afraid that the facts that he discovers in the session might become a dream themselves. The act of covering his eyes suggests there is a visual image. He might want to see what is happening and he might not want the analyst to know he can see it either.

He might also not want to see what is happening; something like not wanting to see things as they are appreciated in a dream and, at the same time, not wanting to see them from an intuitive perspective.

Analyst: I am using the term "see" in the usual sense of insight.

Member: I would like to know Dr Bion's opinion on the idea of immersing oneself in the darkness as a way to see; if, by covering his eyes, the patient might be trying to find some kind of insight or *more* insight.

Dr Bion: Might be. But I consider that one of the difficulties in this session is that the patient is speaking the language of visual imagery and, in that sense, what is happening is that somebody is giving a book to another person, so there is a conversation, but there is also a show; they are two different things; I think the patient has not made up his mind as to whether he wants to know what is happening or whether he wants the analyst to know it. I think the key here is the change of language towards dramatisation and the use of visual imagery.

What are we supposed to pay attention to? To the people having a conversation or to what is happening? If we put ourselves in the observer's place, should we listen to what they are saying or should we see what is happening? What should the analyst in the room interpret, what the patient says or the presentation of the book? In other words, what language must the analyst use? His ears or his eyes?

Analyst: Are they mutually exclusive?

Dr Bion: Unfortunately, they are not.

Analyst: Why unfortunately?

Dr Bion: Because the analyst would be wrong, no matter what he did, if he excluded one or the other. What he is going to do depends on the analyst's opinion about what things are like in that session; he could be using his intuition, his eyes, etc. Another question would be: is the patient using a language that might be obscure, but with the intention of clarifying things as much as possible, or is it a language that makes things as obscure as possible?

The key is that you use your analytical training to shed light on the patient's difficulties; he cannot express what he means, so the analyst must use his intuition and his understanding; free association provides the patient with a means of communication which helps him say what he has to say, if he wants to do it. Interpretation and free association are flawed; you can always question the accuracy of an interpretation. One question is: is the patient speaking about something which is so difficult that he finds it difficult to express, or is it something he does not want the analyst to know and, as a consequence, he makes it as obscure as he can? His presenting the book to the analyst makes me think that it is a bit of both. He seems not to have decided whether he wants to make understanding easier or to make it more obscure.

Clinical material 4

Patient: Since I started individual analysis, things are slowly becoming clearer to me. The other day I was thinking and several images occurred to me; as I am reading and studying, revised images appear; I started associating and I remembered A…

Analyst: It is relevant to clarify that he had studied medicine expecting to become a clinical doctor, and it was when he started working for A, a renowned paediatrician, whose advice he followed, that he decided to become a paediatrician.

Dr Bion: I am starting to feel that this patient is making enormous progress and that he can feel it. That is evidence that the analyst wants to help him. He feels the analyst wants to help him, but he also thinks he might not. He might want to turn him into a paediatrician or into an analyst or who knows what; can he feel safe and continue with his analysis and do his best because he has a good analyst?

From the point of view of the patient, things seem to be getting a bit better; one of the advantages of the progress in his treatment is that it can be used by the patient to be more cooperative. We could say the problem arises when the patient feels worse. Feeling better helps him feel more confident.

Clinical material 5

Patient: A was a really good swimmer; but the kind of swimmer who crosses rivers! He had crossed the Panama gulf several times, he used to do it and he chose the spots where it is really wide, where there are many currents, but he could swim, he knew all the currents. Then I am studying and I feel as if I were crossing the river, with fast strokes, with good breathing, but I am… let's say, I have covered a quarter of the distance more or less and things are going well. I know my limits and I am crossing. I know I am going to cross it, but I have not crossed it yet, and underneath me the river is really deep, then I think the outcome of that crossing is not going to be good, but I must do it! And it scares me.

Analyst: That is precisely your fear, that's why you covered your eyes. That depth represents the conflicts that come to the surface, that must become apparent here; you are feeling that we are not just speaking of swimming on the surface and reaching the other side, but that all that depth can be dangerous. You feel that I am A.

Dr Bion: In such a situation, the patient must do something; he can only do one thing; he can only believe everything is OK. We might be dealing with this patient or we might be dealing with a more complicated case. He imagines there exists something like a good analyst who can understand difficult books, somebody like a good doctor who has reached the other side, like a good swimmer. Could this just be his imagination? In other words: the difficulties he finds in the cure consists in escaping the frustrating situation by believing everything to be OK. The analyst seems to be somebody who can help him, who can understand books and even people, but he does not know if this is true or not because he needs to believe it is so anyway.

One of the disadvantages of using fantasy as a cure is that it worked out for him at one time or another, it saved him from desperation and depression; he reached the other side thanks to his ability to fantasise. It is not easy for us to evaluate the difficulties a bad treatment might present a patient with, but neither could we evaluate a good treatment, because it gives them hope and makes them believe something can be done for them.

Indeed, the patient reads books, he reads people, but does he want to do it? Who is this analyst; father, mother, brother, sister? Reality tells the patient that he is an analyst, but what role is he playing, is he good, is he a bad murderer, does he want to use his knowledge and education to help him? And the patient's crossing the river will depend on all this. *I guess something obvious lies behind all this, the experience of his mother trying to suffocate him. There could be some kind of reminiscence of birth.* It is important for him to ascertain who his analyst is, whether he is his father, mother, etc. But the most important partner he has is the one who shares his body: in other words, it is important for him to learn who he is. This is an idea psychoanalysts have, but I do not think he has reached that point. So the key point is who the people are who can help him to survive, who his analyst is and who he is.

The added complication for the analyst is to know who the patient is dealing with. We are producing some kind of imaginary story, which may help explain what is going to happen; so you can see in the analysis what part of the story becomes apparent and which doesn't; if it doesn't, it means that the story is mistaken, it must be readjusted, and that is the difficulty the analyst must resolve, and he must do it in the analytical situation, in which you cannot think, you cannot afford the luxury of having a battle between your own thoughts.

Member: Dr Bion, how long do you think you can avoid, in a fifty-minute-session, being invaded by these kinds of thoughts which you call either memory or desire?

Dr Bion: I think it is difficult and that you cannot consider yourself to be free of them. You can decide whether you find them useful or not. I am telling you something that has seemed to help me in my experience, but it might not help you; however, it might be worth trying; but I think the situation is not only in your hands. For example, psychotic patients take advantage of the fact that the analyst's ability to forget might temporarily enhance his intuition and understanding, and one of the ties the psychotic will try to break is this one, and he will do so by trying to make you worry about what he said or what you remember, or making you want to cure him. The psychotic patient is some kind of very good and peculiar psychoanalyst; he could have been one of the first psychoanalysts this patient had, at least one who knew how to make him feel awkward. In this regard, I think it is better to try to leave these ideas outside the analytical relation; some patients are not going to help you; on the contrary, they will try to keep their analyst occupied with memories and desires, trying to remember what the patient said in the last session, or trying to remember what the analyst said, or making him feel he has said something wrong or that he has forgotten what the patient said, and while the analyst is busy with that, the patient will move on to something else. Controlling this takes a long time, and you must decide whether you find it useful or not.

Clinical material 6

Patient: Even though it is true that many things are becoming clearer, it is, nonetheless, true that my fears do not disappear. I still feel really afraid; all in all, I think that in these months... well, it is, in truth, another stage to start individual analysis.

Dr Bion: The patient's fears have not disappeared yet. It is difficult to know whether we should interrupt the patient at this stage or not, it depends on what used to happen. Generally speaking, I think it is important to point out to the patient that he is asking the analyst to agree on the need to get rid of his fears, no matter whether they are justified or not. This is another question, because the aim of the analysis is not to reach a point at which the patient no longer feels scared, when he is right to feel scared.

Analyst: I would like you to elaborate a bit more on why you think that patient's fears are justified.

Dr Bion: If he was not scared, he would be dead. If you admit that what you expect is to eliminate fear, the patient can always say: I still feel fear, this proves how bad analysis is. It is not the case so: *you expect the patient to reach a point where fears are just activated when there are good reasons for them*. If you did not have any fears, you would walk down the street and you would be immediately killed.

Analyst: I consider we must make a difference between real fears and neurotic fears.

Dr Bion: All fears are real in some aspects. I agree to make this distinction; when we speak about some kind of neurotic fear, we are speaking about some kind of fear that cannot be explained. *The question is not to get rid of fears; the question is to get rid of that aspect of fear that doesn't have any utility*. This is important because you cannot visualise the moment at which the patient is doing *worse after concluding* the treatment, or *worse than at the beginning* in the sense that you cannot know what his future will be; supposing this patient's future to be a series of disasters of some kind, he should be more conscious instead of less conscious of the nature of these disasters, but we are still dealing with the idea that it is better to be aware of the real reasons for those fears, anxiousness, etc., than to sacrifice that ability to get rid of fears in general.

Member: I would imagine those fears to originate from the patient and from me. On seeing the development of the analysis and on being granted the chance to interpret it, I would do so by understanding the patient's and my own fear of what is happening and of the unknown, but from a technical point of view, I would understand the fear felt by the patient because of what is happening in the analysis. In my formulation, we would find the two people.

Dr Bion: The patient is not usually able to tolerate his own difficulties, that's why he doesn't want to know what his analyst's difficulties are; I think it is reasonable to say you are introducing the patient to himself. The fact that you have to use yourself in this process is irrelevant. I think you can show the patient that he feels you are preoccupied financially, for example, but the key is not whether you are preoccupied, but the fact that the patient is feeling so, and you must show the patient that he is that kind of person. Another patient might not care at all about what is happening to you.

Member: Many of us work with the idea that *a relation is established between the patient and the analyst and that it is impossible to separate the patient's experience from that of the analyst*.

Dr Bion: Obviously you must use all your might. I don't think we must set rules which may tie the analyst's hands in a difficult situation. We must remember that rules can tie his hands. We must grant the patient the chance to project what he needs to project. If the analyst shows too much like he is a person with his own rights, which cannot be denied, though, we would be trying to show an image on a screen that is already occupied by another image. Analysis itself is quite flawed, it introduces sounds, noises that interfere with the patient's thought process. The patient may have some kind of soft spot for the analyst's difficulties and he can mobilise these in such a way that the analyst may lose sight of what is happening because of the distraction. This is especially true of psychotic patients, who get into any kind of trouble so that the analyst cannot concentrate on anything else. On the other hand, we cannot ignore the fact that no relation is so close as the analytical relation is, it is logical for some kind of emotional exchange to exist, but it should not interfere with the patient's freedom, at least in so far as we can avoid it.

Member: What is your opinion of setting? Is *verbal interpretation* the most useful tool in the analytical situation?

Dr Bion: I do not have any opinion about setting. What concerns me is to be allowed to give interpretations; when I feel I am not allowed, I understand the moment has come to set the limits. We can draw the patient's attention to this; for example, if the patient keeps an emotional distance from the analysis, there is no analysis. It is easy for the patient to keep a distance from the analysis and then say that the analysis is worthless, that he has not made any progress. There is a minimum condition for any kind of work and nobody knows what it is, not even the person themselves. Experience in any kind of work you are doing will tell you. As a result of experience, you can know how much you can stand and if the patient, for example, gets himself arrested by the police all the time and the patient is calling the analyst now and again, that patient is doing his best not to let you work. You cannot be fair with your other patients, since even if you are seeing your patient five times a week, he is taking much more of your time than that, he is getting to take big amounts of time from your other patients.

If you are an actor or a singer, it is essential to learn how to express yourself in such a way so as to make yourself heard, to enable people to hear you until the end of the show. If the important thing is your life, you must be perceptible, you must be able to make yourself heard at the end of the race. When people start doing things that interfere with your being heard and you must either shout or give up, you realise you cannot go on like that much longer, *and it is important to be able to set limits, to say: I stop here.* This is especially important when it comes to child analysis, where you must set limits for the child, you must tell him: you cannot go there, or you can do many things but I am not going to let you throw a bottle of ink at me. Some rules must be set.

We expect not to have to do it with adults, except when we are dealing with psychotic patients. You must say, for example, if you are going to let the patient bring a loaded gun to the session. Both extremes are easy to manage, but the kinds of things that become apparent in the analysis are different. I think you must know, and not only through analysis but because of your experience, the conditions that are adequate for us to work well, and that is where it is necessary to set the limit.

With regard to the other question, about verbal interpretation being the most useful tool, I do not think I would try to classify them in a certain order, as I think that *interpretation is a combination of several experiences.* It seems to be so important for the analyst because, to his mind, the interpretation is clear, the work is done even though it might not seem so to the patient, he might need the same thing to be repeated to him several times, on different occasions.

For the analyst, interpretation parallels executive action. This issue about the working conditions works in exactly the same way for the patient. The patient cannot be analysed if he does not come to the session, and he cannot feel his problems if the analyst is bringing his own problems to the work. We must find the best conditions for the analyst to be able to work and for the patient to carry out his task.

(In the following clinical material, the analyst associates something to a dream, so Dr Bion asks him to tell the dream.)

Clinical material 7

Patient: He is in a very big house, on a ground floor. Suddenly he hears loud screaming from upstairs, from the top floor, and he rushes upstairs. He finds a lot of doctors in their white coats; his coat is unbuttoned.

The screaming comes from a toilet; there is some kind of monster banging on the door of this toilet, trying to break it down. This monster has the body of bull and the head of a monkey. He walks upright. When he reaches the monster it moves out, his wife comes out of the toilet and claims the monster wanted to rape her.

Dr Bion: Why do you remember this part of the dream in this moment? What is its relation to this material?

Analyst: It might be related, but I do not know why.

Dr Bion: It does not matter. If you pay attention to the dream, the relation will become apparent. This is what I mean when I use the term "evolution". Listening to what the patient has said and reflecting upon your own free association. The better structured the patient–analyst relationship is, the greater the chance for this to occur, and the analyst will feel more competent as he is the one to remember something important instead of the patient.

Analyst: I might have remembered the dream with regard to the analytical situation we are speaking about. But don't you consider it would also be related to a situation of control, to the "here and now"? I think associations occur all the time, in the session we just create more appropriate conditions for them to happen more easily. What do you think about this?

Dr Bion: That's true, there exists that difficulty. It is like an analytical game; his description of the dream might not be very accurate, the past is forgotten, distorted, and the future has not occurred, so the aim of this game is to exercise our mental muscle; stimulating our mental growth, just like we make games and we do not know what for. There are things people need to forget because they do not need them. I think we must consider these things as a refined adult version of childhood games.

Member: I want to ask about the fear in the patient and in the analyst, and about something Bion said about the setting and the analyst as some kind of god who must bear the idealising projections of the patient. Facing a patient who is afraid, I also feel afraid, is my fear separate from the patient's fear? Telling the patient that I am afraid and that my fear might be his, is an incorrect formulation. Another approach is: the fear you are feeling may extend to me; if this happens, we have two options: either to express it or to keep quiet. The second one implies a greater idealisation of the analyst, the other one diminishes him. Doesn't the level of idealisation required for the therapeutic process to continue depend on each specific case? When this fear appears in the analyst, can't the fact of not including it in the interpretation affect the required level of idealisation in some cases?

Dr Bion: The key is not to let these doubts prevent the analysis in the analytical situation. We are busy introducing the patient to himself. One thing is saying to the patient: at this point, you are not feeling but controlling things so as to turn me into an object in which you place your fears and that way you can leave without them. That depends on whether you agree or not. Something else is: you are scared and so am I; the grounds for the way you are, and the reasons why you are scared, must not affect the patient or what he is doing. Let's observe an extreme case: The patient enters the room and places a gun by his side. It is important to point out to the patient that he is intimidating the analyst so as not to let him make interpretations. The same patient can bring a tuba to the session. This kind of patient finds no difference between a gun, a penknife with which to cut your throat, or a tuba with which he can drown your interpretations. He is simply stopping you. The patient doesn't mind whether you are more scared by a gun than by a tuba. You must ascertain whether the patient is bringing the gun to kill you or to scare you so much that you won't be able to think correctly. The accuracy of your interpretation depends on which of these possibilities you think you are dealing with.

NINTH SEMINAR

The continuation of the case presentation—audience questions

Clinical material 1

Patient: Even though many things are becoming clear, it is also true that my worries have not disappeared yet. I can't deny that I am still afraid. All in all, I think that in these months ... well, in truth, it is starting another stage of individual analysis. From the moment I started individual analysis, things are slowly becoming clearer to me. The other day, I was thinking and different images occurred to me, as I was reading and studying, the images suddenly appeared. I started associating and I remembered A ... (his main paediatric teacher, who talked him into becoming one as well). He was a really good swimmer, the kind of swimmer who crosses rivers! He was a man who had crossed the Parana River routinely. He used to do it, and he chose the places where the river is really wide, where there are many currents, but he could swim, he knew all the currents. Then I am studying and I feel as if I were crossing the river, with fast strokes, with good breathing. I am ... let's say, I have covered a quarter of the distance more or less and things are going well. I know my physical capabilities and I am crossing. I know I am going to cross it, but I have not crossed it yet and the river below me is really deep. Then, I think this crossing is not going to end up well, but I must do it! And that is frightening.

Dr Bion: At this stage, I would feel the patient is frightened of me being the monster and the reason he is afraid is because I am doing analysis to simply turn things more dangerous, to run risks. It is important for the patient to know who his analyst is as he might be useless. This would be danger number one. Danger number two would be for psychoanalysis to be ineffective and then it would become something dangerous and the person who practises it as well. It is important to find out what kind of "bull" the analyst is and why he is running this risk.

Let's try the same story from a different perspective. Let's imagine the patient is becoming anxious. He is afraid his relation with the analyst might be a relation with a colossal, powerful penis, or with a frightening vagina, which might destroy him just like the Parana River might. This would be a much more primitive view than the previous one.

Member: Would this more primitive level be related to birth or the memories of birth?

Dr Bion: I would also like to know that. Bear in mind that this is an analytical game and that its importance does not lie in what happened yesterday, but in what will happen next time. When this idea arises, we must observe this group as if it were just one person. A part of us remembers a dream, another part wonders if it will be related to birth; what matters is whether the patient feels there is going to be a birth. Again, that can be seen as something primitive, for example, if the analyst is pregnant or if he might have to be or if it is just one of so many rebirths that we can witness throughout our lives in which one emerges from a mental state to another or is drowned in his previous state.

Analyst: I mentioned in the material that he is an only child. This week, between the previous presentation and this one, he has spoken to me about his sister for the first time. I was extremely surprised, as he had never mentioned her.

Dr Bion: What I understand is that if the analysis develops in such a way that it leads to the growth and evolution of the patient, things that had never been mentioned before will become apparent. Now, there is a sister. This explains why we are getting entangled with a birth, and not just that; there must be a pregnant mother somewhere and a dangerous father in his record. It does not matter whether he had not mentioned his sister before; what matters is that the analysis progresses. The key here is why the patient feels able to tell you now and not why he had not mentioned it before. I am starting to think that soon, we will be wondering why that baby does not have a penis. Could he have been perhaps cleansed, adrift in urine, and if so, by whose urine? The father's, the mother's, or the all-powerful child's? I would like to remind you that we are building a model that I hope all of us will forget so as to let the patient express his mind. This is only helpful for us to listen to the patient.

Clinical material 2

Patient: I know my physical capabilities and I am crossing. I know I am going to cross it, but I have not crossed it yet and the river below me is really deep. So, my chances of crossing are good, but I still must do it! And that is frightening.

Analyst: That is fear, that is why you have covered your eyes. All that depth represents the problems which must come to the surface here. You feel it is not just crossing to the other side, but that the depths can be very dangerous. You feel that I am an analyst, that I know all the secrets of the depths, and, as a result, I am almighty and that's why I am not going to be able to appreciate your efforts and I might refuse to help you reach the psychoanalytical shore.

Patient: Yes, it is something like that: as I set to studying, I can see myself crossing the river at ease.

Analyst: Studying is represented by swimming across the river, but on the surface, and here we realise that apart from studying you must be analysed and that is the dangerous and painful depth.

Patient: Yes, that frightens me.

Analyst: You are saying: "That frightens me", and you are covering your eyes again.

Dr Bion: I think he is cheating because thanks to the analysis he can feel he runs no risk of losing his penis, being suffocated, or becoming a girl. He can see himself swimming well. This is one of those situations in which fantasy is important. If you are feeling helpless, scared, you can imagine the situation is good and you will survive. The disadvantage is that it also works the other way round. When things are going really well, you cannot know if this is a fact or if we would believe it anyway. Let's consider the same possibility, but applying more refined analytic terms. We can say that this patient feels that his relation with his analyst leads him to believe that analysis is no nonsense. Hence, he feels reaffirmed, in a sense: the analysis can work. But if this is true, then anything can happen. He can be afraid of your sexual attack. He might be scared that, within a process which is supposed to be therapeutic, he might be drowned by his unconscious; or that conscience might rule to a point in which his unconscious might disappear. Both are scary situations. Not having any imagination, irrational thought, or fantasy is really serious, but so is living in an imaginary world. The feeling of the existence of a birth about to happen might be related to his feeling; it is good to have some relation with the unconscious or to his feeling that it might be best to keep the unconscious separate from the conscious.

In more elaborate terms, the analyst might say that this patient is unable to decide whether to run towards his cure, whether to become a doctor, paediatrician, psychoanalyst, to get as far as possible from the scene of birth, from his parents' sexual intercourse, or to decide to make a massive regression to his childhood. I do not see this as some kind of underlying desire, but I think it is important to bear it in mind as a psychoanalytical technique and a terminology with which to consider this aspect from an abstract perspective, whether we are dealing with this patient or not, extending it to other patients whose danger is more acute.

Member: Could this be related to the "catastrophic change"?

Dr Bion: No, but in this sense, as you have brought it up, we might wonder if analysis is not carried out by basing ourselves on several catastrophes rather than on some kind of slow growth. We take for granted that time is essential for the analysis, it is like childhood. The human animal is that kind of animal; it takes a long time to mature, but whether changes are slow or not, that is a different matter. When a child says: "Oh, I understand now what you said, I did not know what you meant", that is sudden understanding. On the other hand, the fact that interpretations must be so often repeated implies that understanding takes time. We have an important aspect left that sooner or later will have to be dealt with by the psychoanalyst; it reminds me of another unsolved problem that has to do with light transmission. The quantum theory and the undulating theory, apparently incompatible, but both true up to the moment. Here, both catastrophic changes and gradual changes appear to be the same thing. All this question of growth seems to give mathematicians a lot of trouble. It is taking too long to look at it from a mathematical perspective. I think this is notorious in the child; he can notice the food he ingests is related with his faeces, with what he destroys, but it takes him a long while to realise that his growth is related to what he eats. Why the analytical process is related to the growth of the human being is a mystery.

TENTH SEMINAR

Bion's Analytical Supervision: Jorge, an adolescent analysand—audience questions

Background

Jorge is seventeen and a half years old. He started his treatment in September 1962. He is the eldest of five siblings. He experienced trauma during birth, with suffocation and the use of forceps, as the umbilical cord was wrapped around his neck. He was circumcised seven days after his birth, according to Jewish ritual. His younger brother was born just two days before Jorge's first birthday; for that reason, the patient was weaned by his pregnant mother when he was three months old.

When he was a baby, his parents travelled abroad, and he was left in the care of his grandparents; then his mother came back for him and he moved to another country with his parents and brother. At the age of three, he started to speak. He was always a "reserved and isolated" child; he did not play with his brothers and he hardly spoke.

During his treatment, he was involved just in drawing for years. Nowadays, he speaks in an informational way, and once the first twenty minutes of the session have passed, he drifts into periods of deep silence or "misty areas" (a term that appeared in a science fiction novel he spoke of in one session).

Despite his favourable evolution within his household, his studies, and in his relations with others, I don't feel satisfied because I have not managed to penetrate what happens in that "misty area". At his parents' request, the patient will interrupt his treatment at the end of the year.

As is usual in treating adolescents, Jorge kept his materials in a basket. In March, I told him that by the end of June I would remove it, and this was the last session in which the basket was present.

This session was tape-recorded. We have been recording the patient's sessions for years.

Jorge's session: Saturday, 29 June 1968

Patient: Yesterday, one of my mother's friends came home to teach me to draw a little, perspective and all that stuff. I am going to attend her lessons every Saturday after my session. Her place is very near here; I think it is near Plaza Italia. She told me that I drew quite well, that I had my own style. Yesterday, I was drawing, I made two pyramids, yes, some kind of pyramids like these, that join, and then I coloured the background. When I was about to colour the background, Guillermo called me. He told me that the Bee-Gees' long play had been released. My mother lent me some money and I rushed to buy records, then I listened to them at night and they were fantastic.

Analyst: I think you are telling me that starting your drawing lessons makes you happy, you think it is fantastic, just like the records, because right now you can use it to make up for the drawings you are not going to make here any more.

Patient: No, right now, I do not like it much, because she said that first I was going to start drawing still-life a bit and then I will draw perspective, which is a killjoy, it's crap!

Analyst: I guess you are telling me that my pointing out to you the death or the end of a stage in your analysis, which was drawing, is "crap". You consider having to think about that a "killjoy", you would like to move on to other things straight away, and not to speak about that any more as if it did not exist.

Patient: Yesterday, I went to visit the faculty, the entrance examination is in March or February, at the end of February or in the first days of March. So I am going to start preparing myself for it, I don't know, next month, not yet. (Pause)

Analyst: See how you did not like my interpretation and you just moved on to your future plans, what's more, you left today's session which means more or less the end of a stage and you moved onto February, that is the end of the analysis, after the interruption; as that time is much further away, what you feel is less intense.

Patient: Yesterday, I did not have class because a teacher had died. On my way to school, I bumped into some boys who were on their way back. I asked: had somebody died and was there no school today? (he laughs) Then the headmaster said that a teacher had died.

Analyst: Yes, somehow the idea is that today is the last day we are going to have the basket, and that represents death for me; for you it is like a party, like when a teacher dies and there is no school; I mean, I represent the part of you that has to feel, that has to feel it as death, as separation. In truth, you are saying: well, it does not matter, this disappears, "I have the Bee-Gees, the new things, I have other things, this does not interest me any more; I have another drawing teacher, everything is solved."

Patient: (Long pause) … The Bee-Gees have a song in which they are just, it is, it is a song by Beethoven, where the man is speaking and the orchestra is backing him, because the guys have a complete orchestra.

Analyst: At this point, you are taking some distance. I have made two or three interpretations from the beginning so I have become dangerous. Then you have taken some distance, you have played the record, and now the two of us are listening to the record. If I turn on the recorder, you turn on the record player, then we make the recorder listen to a record. The point is that if I listen to the recording later it will be as if I were listening to records, I will not be listening to you as you are not there. I mean, the real Jorge, the other Jorge, the one in the "misty area" is not there.

Patient: I think I am going to Ana Maria's place today at seven, with *el Gordo*. We will have to travel for at least thirty-five minutes, to Belgrano, maybe farther away. Then, at about 9:30, I have to go back to Julia's, to her wedding. Afterwards, if my parents are not around, and if I stay a little at the wedding, I will go back to Ana Maria's place; but if I leave the wedding at twelve or so, I will go home to sleep, I reckon. (Pause) Today, I have to wear the stupid suit, ha. (He laughs.) (Pause)

Analyst: (I seem to awaken.) I think you are living my interpretations as the demand to wear a suit, as if you were concluding from my interpretations that I demand that you work seriously, as if I made you wear formal clothes, like a suit.

Patient: The suit, for example, looks better when the trousers are tight. Then a four-buttoned fitted jacket, and then who knows, a flowery or frilled shirt, and a flowery tie.

Analyst: You are telling me that you have adjusted a Jorge who is to be looked at but not to feel touched. If I just limit myself to looking at you and not connect with you, then, we can say we are even.

Patient: (Short pause) Today I had a dream, I do not know if I was Tarzan's son, or if another guy was Tarzan's son, but it was set in modern times; the guy was captured with a girl, after which the two of them escaped in a car. They drove out of a garage and then they drove away and I do not know what else happened. (Pause. I feel surprised because this is his third or fourth dream in almost seven years of treatment.) On the cover of the album, one of the members of the Bee-Gees is wearing a wonderful shirt with a long collar and a striped green and yellow tie; they have that at Modart (a store for fashionable "mod" clothing). (Pause)

Analyst: You might be trying to dream instead of drawing. Obviously, in your dream about Tarzan, you are Tarzan's son, even though you do not know if it was you or another person, and in your dream you are persecuted, you are running away because you are being persecuted. And I understand you might be running away from me, from being able to sit on the coach, or being able to use the desk to draw on. It makes you distrust me, it makes us enemies. And you have to feel omnipotent, like

Tarzan, so as to feel that you can oppose me, and that's why you might be trying to change from drawing to dreaming.

Patient: I am not going to have my hair cut until next week, that is if the hairdresser comes, and then I will not have my hair cut again for another month. (Pause)

Analyst: You are saying that you are going to have your hair cut next week and that then you are not going to have it cut again for another month; you said it a bit fast, like saying, in a sense, that you are not going to let me make a mess of your head, to make cuts in your head or to make you feel some kind of emptiness, to make you feel there is something missing. That is, the one who has to feel the basket missing is me, I am the one who has to feel worried about it.

Patient: I had already given up the basket some time ago, more or less when I started sitting down, sitting here on the couch.

Analyst: As you are secretly telling me you had given up the basket some time ago, you are telling me that you had already prepared yourself for this moment, without letting me know about it. You got ahead of the feeling of emptiness you might feel today. On the other hand, as a result of your fear of becoming weak, in the sense of showing your feelings, you must turn into a character like Tarzan, Tarzan's son, somebody who is very strong, omnipotent, somebody who is not affected by this kind of things, very macho. We have seen on many occasions that you identify feelings with being effeminate, so you must be somebody considered to be very macho, like Tarzan who has long hair but is very macho. (Pause of over five minutes)

Analyst: Now you have entered the "misty area", and that way we are in a different stage, I mean, you brought a dream, you gave it to me to ponder over, you got rid of it quickly, you left it to me. Now I have to ponder over it, I have to interpret it. You brought the dream to me in order to make up for "well, I am not going to have a basket any more", and because you were afraid of what I could do with something like this, something different like a dream, of which we have had very few in the course of the analysis, and then you enter your "misty area" and you leave me alone, just me and the recorder.

Patient: (Five minutes in silence. When he speaks, he startles me as if he woke me up all of a sudden.) There was a part in the dream, I think I was being tortured. And then, when the guy left, my hands and feet were tied, I just did this and they were freed, then…

Analyst: What, what?

Patient: I do this and they are free.

Analyst: No, what was happening at the beginning?

Patient: Another guy was torturing me.

Analyst: Were you torturing yourself?

Patient: No, a guy was torturing me, he was beating me, he had tortured me, I reckon. Then, afterwards, when I run away, I think I take a horse or I do not know what, and I think I said, no, that it was better, and then they quickly brought me a car, quickly, a jeep.

Analyst: You thought that a car was better and they drove you fast in a jeep?

Patient: Yes. (Pause)

Analyst: I think this dream is connected to the fact of giving up the basket and having to speak. It is understood as a torture, a persecution, and well, you have to escape from it somehow, you have to find a mechanism to escape, because not even silence is perfect as a mechanism any more because each session I can overcome it, and I can get you out of your "misty area", and then you feel the dream and you try to find another way out. However, by bringing me a dream, I think it is the third in the whole course of the treatment, and as it has been a long time since you brought me a dream, you might be asking me to contain you, because even though a part of you is trying to escape, there is another part that comes here, that takes it seriously, and that is asking me not to let the other Jorge run away, because, well, he realises it is a lie, letting the other Jorge escape is deceiving the two of you. That might be the reason for your bringing me a very peculiar message today, a special present, the dream.

Patient: (Really long pause) All my nose is full of pus, that's why I have so many pimples.

Analyst: All your nose is full of pus?

Patient: Yes, that's why I was doing this in any pore and a trickle of pus comes out. (Pause)

Analyst: Any time you speak, I have to ask you what you are saying, I mean, you entered your "misty area" a little, but you come out like this, and at times quickly. You are silent and then suddenly you speak, you say something fast and then go back to your silence. You are forcing me to make an effort to listen to you, and then, in that way, I have to listen but I cannot think about what you say because my effort must be aimed at listening to you. You might have changed your strategy, that is, for you, squeezing your mind, and getting out some of those thoughts that flow into the misty area is like getting pus out, because that is the part you are afraid of or the part you consider to be ailing, crazy, like pus. (Really long pause)

Analyst: You are silent because you are in a "misty area" and you cannot rescue yourself from there, because, as we saw the other day, in the "misty area" there were prehistoric animals that attacked the cars, in the story?

Patient: Well, yes, but they were some big guys.

Analyst: Pardon?

Patient: Some kind of robots, very big, they spat fire, I think.

Analyst: When you enter that area, you encounter those prehistoric animals or robots, who spit fire, big beings, that is, horrific terrifying things. Then the way to avoid that is by avoiding me because, otherwise, the demand of staying awake, and of letting that come out becomes excessive, and that makes you anxious (he was moving in the chair) because of what we analyse. However, if I enter the "misty area", then you feel more relaxed, but today I did not enter the "misty area" either and that's why you are feeling bad. Yesterday, at this point of the session and with this same sequence of events, you were the one who was falling asleep; today, you have not fallen asleep, but you are feeling anxious, uncomfortable, and you feel like leaving. (Really long pause)

ELEVENTH SEMINAR

The continuation of an adolescent case presentation—audience questions

Dr Bion: What does that mean, the Bee-Gees?

Translator: They are a music band.

Analyst: He used to draw all the time, now records have become the centre of his life, his big aim in life is to become a disc-jockey.

Dr Bion: This raises the *issue of recording the sessions*. The usual idea in England is to not use a recorder because it affects both the analyst and the person being analysed, disturbing the situation to a great extent. In order to preserve the analytical situation, the analyst must be like a blank screen, capable of receiving the patient's projections. In truth, this is never entirely achieved, obviously, there are always distortions; there are distortions in the interpretations that are not given and in those that are given. I think the recorder must be taken into account in analysis, and in this analysis I think it is an important tool. In my opinion, both with regard to the basket and to the recorder, we must consider the patient's reaction, and, in this case, the patient perceives the analyst as if he were pregnant; and the basket and the recorder are considered as objects that are present. There are three people in the room. However, these fantasies would have turned up in the analysis anyway, there can always be something that can *lead the patient to believe that the analyst is pregnant*.

Analyst: The recorder has been used for three years. At the beginning of the treatment, Jorge hardly spoke, and then he started speaking in a very confusing way, that's why I found it impossible to understand if I did not use a recorder.

Another member: To my mind, the recorder constitutes making objective what he calls memory and desire, the way in which he deals with countertransference reactions from a technical perspective.

Dr Bion: I think that what interests us is what he manages, what is being managed, and what the patient thinks he is managing. Recording the sessions is not the challenge, the difficulty lies in the fact that recording the sessions is an obstacle, from the analytical perspective.

Dr Bion: I consider that the patient can hear the recorder, and the recorder interrupts the conversation between the patient and the analyst, with its sounds, it is playing Beethoven. Another aspect is that the recorder appears like the mother when she was pregnant, and she could not hear what the baby said before it was born. It is complicated because she does not know that she is in the "misty area" and she cannot hear what the baby is saying.

Analyst: Is the "misty area" the baby speaking from the mother's womb?

Dr Bion: That must be taken into account all the time, because it is not something static, he might not see that you are pregnant, he might not see the interior of the mother, he might not see the baby, but he can listen, he knows what you are saying, he has felt the baby. There are two different stories about the same facts.

Dr Bion: Why does he laugh?

Analyst: He is laughing because as he has to go to the wedding of some friends of his parents, he has to dress smartly, he has to wear a suit like us. He is usually dressed like a hippie in all kinds of colours and his parents did not allow him to go to the wedding dressed like that. He had to wear a suit and, when he said he had to wear a suit, he laughed.

Dr Bion: I think the important point here is that he is expressing the fact that the baby is born in the wedding. The wedding is an event at which objects gather and in the meantime the baby is born. He, then, can see it. He claims he knows what is happening in that moment; he knows the analyst is pregnant, he knows the analyst has a relation with another object. One of the difficulties in this sense is that the baby can be heard, but he cannot hear what it is saying; there are two different stories. The only way out he has is to wear the horrible suit, the suit or your state of mind is like the other side of the skin, which enables him to be present. Behind this lies the feeling that he should know how babies are born, because he has been born so he could see how it was done; but he has forgotten it, that resides in the "misty area". The next baby, the next patient, whoever it is, will know that, and he envies the baby that knows much more than he does about this question. He has missed his opportunity, he was offered the chance to learn everything about this, and he feels envy. But the next baby knows the answer. And to be able to learn the answer, he will have to wear the horrible suit, whatever that is. Admittedly, obviously it is not a good state of mind, it is a different state of mind, it is a horrible state of mind, to equal the baby who knows more. It is in a more sophisticated way, his brother and himself are going to the wedding, but his brother knows what happens at the wedding. I am not really sure if it is the brother; somebody knows it. I think it is the brother who knows it; the brother is also an aspect of himself. There was a time when he was the brother and he knew it, and the one who knew how babies are born is not there any more. And to know this, he will have to wear his dead Self, his horrible Self, in order to know. This is based on his feeling, not that he learned something in the analysis or that he learned something in his childhood, but that he knew everything about weddings and so on, but in order to leave behind his old personality, his horrible personality, he got rid of everything he had learned at his parents' wedding, when his parents got married and they made him, they let him look. In other words, he feels he was cured when he left behind that horrible Self, but he got rid of that horrible Self in such a violent way that he also got rid of everything that horrible Self knew. One of the complications is that this is very compact, we have him before existing; himself, who existed when his brother was born; himself in his brother when he was born, and it is a horrible part, a part that is bigger now, it must be because he got rid of it, of this horrible part. The only reason for getting rid of this bad part of himself is that it is bad; he dissociates from it and gets rid of this part which is too bad. But in this case, it is the bad part of himself, the horrible state of mind, the hippie state of mind, whatever that is. Yet, the horrible part he has got rid of becomes worse, because he has got rid of it. This is based on his feeling of not wanting to be rejected. Hence, if he is responsible for rejecting a part of himself because of its wickedness, then he thinks it has become worse because it was rejected by him. This is based on the observation, both of himself and of remains of his old Self and of his brother, and of the anxiety he feels at seeing how horrible babies are. This is also based on feeling that a child's birth is similar to the evolution of emotional experience, and emotion itself is similar to a horrible baby. I understand that here we can also find a reminiscence of the emotion the baby feels; it is felt as a horrible baby, the bad baby, not the good baby, like the one the mother produces.

I would like to switch to another topic for a second. I would like to reflect on the status of what this seminar is. I think it should be considered some kind of game that we play. It should have the quality of the games played during our childhood, and it derives from them. The same proportion of entertainment and earnestness, like in children's games. This is not a post-mortem of analytical sessions; we are using the analytical session to build a model for our future use. Something similar to when children pretend to be parents, in order to build a pattern to use when they really become parents. But this is in the shorter term. We are making a model to use in tomorrow's session, in the day after tomorrow's session, not any later. But for all these reasons, even though I think we must regard what we are doing in earnest, I also think we must forget it, because the question here is using this game, which is similar to doing some kind of mental exercise; we are doing what a child does while playing, but the session is completely different. The rehearsal is different from the thing it represents. The game is different from what it prepares us for. I am trying to evaluate the scientific status of this meeting. It is not a description of what happened in the analytical session, nor is it a description of what is going to happen; it is neither a memory nor a prediction of the future. It must be forgotten, because nothing can come between the analyst and the patient's expression.

I am including this because I understand that it is necessary to have an idea of the state of our thinking, so as to not have the wrong idea, about whether it is a report of what happened or a prediction for the future. However, our memories are distortions of the past, and our predictions are equally false, because we do not know what may happen. But the key is to find a procedure which enables us to have an open attitude, so that there cannot exist "misty areas". We can resume the analysis and proceed; this is the advantage of this kind of game.

I consider it is a description of the analysis. He is using it to describe a situation in which the analytical game, which he considers to be some kind of repetition of his own problems, is not satisfactory because it is too theoretical. The analyst formulates his interpretations and the patient must generate associations, which are, in a sense, theories. Instead of speaking about weddings and about how babies are born, it would be better to play a sexual game together, instead of speaking about that. It would be nicer if he had a shirt with flowers in the chest, if he had a penis, which is also a flower, then he would be able to play a game which is very interesting and he would feel well.

I think he considers the analysis to be too theoretical, too abstract, and it might not be too similar to a game with his brother; it would be better if the analyst were like his brother and they could play together, and play a very nice game, a nice sexual game, about babies, weddings, etc. Does anyone want to discuss these points? Because I think it is very important for us to explore our minds about these issues.

Question 1

Are interpretations very abstract or is the patient too concrete? You would interpret the concreteness of his thought, the specific action, for the patient instead of the association; are we dealing with a flaw of the analyst or with a flaw of the thought of the person analysed because of his inability to abstract? How would you cope with this from a technical perspective?

Dr Bion: I consider that in analysis, it is wise to keep existing procedures. The only thing we can do is formulate interpretations, at a theoretical level. In truth, the patient's associations are equally theoretical, they are a theoretical way to express feelings.

Question 2

As the analyst interprets one thing and the patient says another, because he does not want words, but rather a sexual relation, is it a flaw in the thinking of the person being analysed that you would take into account from a technical perspective?

Dr Bion: No, I wouldn't. I think it is different. I think the patient is also theoretical, and the analyst wouldn't be able to say, well, let's masturbate or pleasure ourselves, or something similar; that is out of the question. In truth, here there are his stories. It is not just the analyst, or Freud, who wants the analysis to be a theoretical discussion and to keep it at that level, but that the patient wouldn't be able to stand it if they acted on it. The analyst knows it, but the patient doesn't. There are patients who try to do it, who try to turn the analysis into a sexual relation; generally speaking, they try to actualise the interpretations, but if they did, they would not like it. They try to actualise a sexual game, and then they would overreact. But what happens with this patient, is that he considers the analysis to be too theoretical, and the patient also feels that it is like a sexual game, he even thinks that the theoretical conversation is sexual. The idea is to make it closer, not just to feel it like a sexual game but to turn it into a sexual game. But he would not be able to bear it.

Analyst: On many occasions, I felt that his emotional blockage was due to the fact that he felt my interpretations as some kind of homosexual intercourse, and then he blocked himself constantly so as not to let me enter.

Dr Bion: Indeed, especially at his age. It would be wise to think that when the patient hears what you are saying, keeping an idea in his mind can be considered a sexual act, and this can give way to some dangers, if this aspect is not understood and if it is not explained to the patient. The patient can accuse the analyst of having carried out a sexual relation.

Analyst: His worry about the recorder, about the baby, can it be related to the fact that his mother endured many abortions and he has a deceased brother?

Dr Bion: No, not up to where we have got so far. The way in which I would deal with this, would be considering that this analytical game is similar to the analysis. You can have been analysing and suddenly this idea comes to your mind, you may not have thought about it from the beginning of the analysis, but it appears in your mind just like it came up in this discussion. It is what I call evolution, it flows during the discussion. I may think I had forgotten it, that I had not heard anything about this, that I did not know anything; this is what should happens in analysis. You don't have to worry about memories, but to find something close in your mind. You always feel, and you might be right, that you should remember everything. I do not think so. You must let the analytical situation bring it up at the opportune moment. At this stage, nothing about the abortions has appeared, but we do not know what can happen later. That's why it is important to forget everything, and to let abortions appear, if they do, or the deceased brother. But if they do not appear, they must not be included.

Question 3

Would you take it into account if you are working this way and suddenly you remember it?

Dr Bion: Indeed, I consider you must show the utmost respect for the session.

Analyst: The parents told me, he didn't, that's why I did not include it.

Question 4

Even if the patient does not bring it, if it flows in his mind, would you include it?

Dr Bion: There is no such thing as the "patient". We use these terms such as psychoanalysis, patient, analyst, person undergoing analysis, but there are real people and real situations which approximate the theory. The theory is a generalisation, it can be good or not, but tomorrow's session is quite real, and the fact that there are two people in the room is quite real. I do not think you can separate easily patient and analyst;

when two people share a relationship, it is very difficult to know who contributes what. The only reason why we can attribute it to the person undergoing the analysis is because we do not know what the husband and the wife contribute, we can just get close to it. In analysis, there are two people, and nothing must come between them. The closer we get to the situation, the more difficult it becomes to claim that it is just the analyst who thinks so. They probably contribute something, their memories and desires, but we can consider that these ideas come from the person undergoing the analysis. The better we know ourselves, the easier it is to say: "Yes, I have this idea, but the patient has done something for me to have it." It is a two-person duty, not one.

Question 5

Another member: What you call evolution is what we call countertransference reaction, it is just a semantic question.

Dr Bion: It is a semantic question, but in truth it is as follows: theoretically, semantically, countertransference is unconscious; hence, we do not know what we feel, it affects the analysis because it is something unconscious, and there is no way to deal with this other than to submit yourself to analysis. However, you cannot be analysed while you are analysing; then countertransference becomes an obstacle. If you know that you are angry or furious with the patient, I do not think that can be called, from a technical perspective, countertransference, I think that is something we can work with. But, due to its being unconscious, countertransference cannot be used in the analysis. If we use the word "countertransference", it is important from scientific and semantic perspectives to realise that we are using a theory as a model for something else. One of the difficulties we face is that we must be really precise; I think it is something that adds up to all our other problems, giving things their proper name. It is useful to keep to definition and, if necessary, to create a new term. The problem arises when we discover new things and we need new terms. For our theoretical contributions, it is better to keep to the primitive meaning; we cannot use a different language each time.

PART V

BION'S DIALOGUE WITH THE AUDIENCE ON QUESTIONS ABOUT SUPERVISION

TWELFTH SEMINAR

Dr Bion's supervisory comments*—on the analyst's capacities for observation, formulation, and interpretation—audience questions

Dr Bion: I would like to highlight the fact that we already have the observations made by the analyst so we are assuming limited scope. Supervision belongs to what I call analytical game, and I'd rather understand all the psychoanalytical training as a game. It makes us anxious just in the ways games made us anxious in our childhood, but we also find it reassuring because it offers us something to rely on. Obviously, reality is very different, one thing is playing to be a mum or a dad and another thing is being one. What we are doing here is very different from what we will later do with the patient in our offices.

I would like to elaborate on this aspect: the moment in which you get to make an interpretation is rather unimportant, as that interpretation is the consequence of days, months, weeks, even years, of experience. When an interpretation can be given, when all that hazy material can be formulated, and formulated in such a way that the patient can understand it, the analytical work is really made. It would be nice to be able to sit down and admire the good work both of us have carried out, but analysis is not like that, because as soon as you make an

---

*This supervision corresponds to 31 July 1968. The clinical material has been eliminated as Dr Bion's interventions are clear enough.

interpretation, the situation changes and there is no time to appreciate our good luck.

I would also like to add that all interpretation interferes in the analysis, and it also interferes in the analyst's observations, we cannot avoid it. In his *Autobiography*, Charles Darwin claims that he cannot judge and observe at the same time, I think he is right, but I also think we should do it anyway. It would be convenient and it would help the outcome of the task, if you could make the interpretation almost absent-mindedly, so attention wouldn´t be diverted from what is happening. That is, the analyst must be all the time open to the affective experience that is taking place in each moment, even when an interpretation is being made. The material that will one day lead to an interpretation is being given all the time, perhaps tomorrow, next week, or the following year; *so, it is essential for the analyst to make as few interruptions as possible, so as to be able to absorb the emotional involvement*. That's why I think it is important to be able to make an interpretation, as I said before, absent-mindedly, so as not let it interfere with the acquisition of more information. We must admit that even if we do not understand, even if we feel confused, this is an essential part of the analytical process; what an analyst needs is not just to make questions but to be able to put up with half-truths, mistakes, doubts, hesitation. I might be quoting Keats.

Question 1

You have said that before interpreting a patient's difficulty (like reading a book or reading music), it is useful to know well where the difficulty resides, and following with the idea of each interpretation being an interruption in the process, *what is your opinion of the questions that the patient might be asked* to help us shed us light on the difficulty the patient is speaking about?

Dr Bion: I think that when the analysis has already been in progress for a while, the patient might be able to answer questions, sometimes they can even do it at quite an early stage of the analysis; it depends on the patient. What I sometimes ask is: "What is your difficulty with the book?", or something like that. The patient may answer: "That's your business, not mine", or just say he doesn't know. All in all, I would say: "I asked a question, you may answer, that would save us time; if you can't, we will have to find another way", and I would leave it like that. It is a matter of opinion, but it is true we do not know what a patient is capable of, he might be able to answer a direct question, or he might not and he might just be able to answer by using free association. In short, sometimes we get an answer, maybe we get a hostile answer, and other times we see that associations give an unexpected turn and then we can say: "Now you are answering the question I made you and which you were unable to find an answer to earlier, and now you are giving me the answer", and in that moment we can make an interpretation.

Question 2

In my opinion, when we are working with patients who are progressing well, after quite a long time of analysis, where almost all the process is spontaneous, interpretation is an interruption; in that situation, I think that the analyst's intervention might be described as punctuating the patient's language. Sometimes you just need to clear your throat to encourage him, others you just need to repeat the last sentence he said. What is your opinion of this technique?

Dr Bion: Sometimes, the archaeologist who works with his spade and his pick until he finds an object and then continues with his brush made of camel's hair serves as a model for this situation; in analysis the situation is similar: how can we make an interpretation without disrupting facts? That is really difficult.

There is another issue whose relevance I am not really sure of. In my opinion, we can obtain reassurance of an interpretation if you explain or seem to explain what has happened up to that point, if you show the form; but if that interpretation sheds light on what has not happened yet, it will be more valuable. In other words, an interpretation that aims at shedding light on the events that are taking place can also be used to shed light on events or facts that have not become apparent yet, that have not happened yet. This can be applied to all the analysis. We can feel the analysis as a rewarding experience, and it should not be partly rewarding; if you feel that you have managed to make the patient understand something, and as a result you have also learned more about patients that you will be able to apply in the future, then we can guess the analysis was a good analysis.

Question 3

What is your opinion of the use of metaphors to express what is taking place in the session, for example "chain reaction"; do you think a plastic representation like that is useful, or is it better to use the same words the patient employs?

Dr Bion: That does not worry me. I feel I have the right to have bad habits, and I consider everybody has the right to say which they are. But the problem is this: we are dealing with such an urgent situation that I do what I can. I think my duty is not being an analyst or a good analyst, but just trying to be one. For me, the point is not to let time drift away. My concern is to absorb what is happening and just say what I can, as simply and as fast as I can, with the hope of having grown habits that make me feel I can be quite expressive. I do not mind much its not being so, or that these flaws appear, because I hope to use them in the analysis without causing much trouble. On the other hand, I think I would be causing more trouble if I had to worry about how I was going to formulate what I have to say. I think that at the beginning of our analytical career, we must pay attention to this aspect of formulation; what's more, I don't think we can afford to be men of science, or artists, since we have to be both things. If we can find an aesthetically satisfactory way to express what must be said, and if we have grown that habit at an early stage, even better; at a later stage you cannot afford to worry about that.

I would like to turn that statement around and apply it to the patient. We must bear in mind the following situation: the patient tells us he has had a dream and he starts telling us about his dream. The analyst must wonder: is the patient telling me a dream or is he telling me what happened at the weekend? Why is he telling me? Is it because it is the fastest, shortest, and clearest way of communicating he can make use of? Or is it because it is the longest, the most dubious, and the most controversial? This is a key aspect, because it is necessary to tell the patient what he is doing.

Just like the analyst, the patient should be trying to express himself in the clearest way possible; the shortest and clearest way might be telling his dream, then he should tell it, but he shouldn't do it when it is the most obscure way and the easiest to reject, by alleging that it is just an interpretation.

This might be clearer if we take the problem to the field of literature. When it comes to an obscure poem, the poet might have written it so because he thought he should do it that way, if its obscurity was the best the poet could do, then that is true poetry. The same applies to analytical works, where this problem of communication is vital. The articles on psychoanalysis that are obscure, dubious, etc. can help show how intelligent the author is, or they might be the shortest and clearest way to speak about a topic which is, in itself, obscure. That is what we must decide.

THIRTEENTH SEMINAR

Dr Bion's supervisory comments*—on questions regarding the patient's repetition compulsion—symbiotic relationships—the analytic contract—audience questions

Question 1

Given the case material we have seen, we can appreciate the ambivalence that had already become apparent in the previous session, shouldn't we examine that repetition compulsion?

Dr Bion: I would like to draw your attention to this issue. I think terms like "repetition compulsion" are terms we use here in these kinds of discussions, but we should avoid them when speaking to the patient. From an analytic perspective, we could say that if this patient cannot be analysed, then his only cure might be the repetition of the episode. Whichever it is, he feels hopeless and obligated to do so because he has no other hope. This usually happens when patients do not believe in psychoanalysis; it becomes another episode of their repetition compulsion. *I am not devaluing the term "repetition compulsion", but we need to change our theoretical formulation into something more pictorial, and the pictorial is more abstract and we need to get used to these exercises in their twofold nature of transformation.* For example, speaking about this patient, what prevails, what is

*7-8-1968.

repeated, is his permanent need for someone to be near him. However, not even in the case of the baby must the mother be there all the time.

Question 2

From the perspective of a symbiotic relationship, don't you think the relief the patient expresses comes as a result of the analyst seeing him at his scheduled time?

Dr Bion: Indeed, the patient thinks that if he had managed to tie up the analyst, he would have had problems in the future. In the original situation, this is unknown, because a baby is not experienced enough to know that it is not good when his mother gives in and allows herself be attacked by her son to the point at which she does not dare leave her baby alone. This will make the baby unable to set his own independence in the future because of his guilt. So I agree there exists a therapeutic element which is difficult to identify in the analysis. We don't know why people get better as a result of the analysis; however, this kind of thing might be helpful. It is not convenient that the analyst submits to blackmail. He might have to do it, because patients get to control the situation and you feel forced to do things that you know are wrong from an analytical perspective. However, it is not good to do so, it doesn't help the analyst nor the patient, even when it could mean a temporary impasse. That's why I agree that, in this case, it might have had a therapeutic effect. Keep to this, with your sessions, your interruptions, in the way you combine them. Try not to start seeing a patient before a long interruption, because there is not enough time for the patient to be able to bear it; it is always better to accept a patient at the beginning of the year.

I think it is important to pay attention to the following issue: let's see everything as a completely new situation. That's what I have already said, as if you are seeing a new patient in each session, not the one you saw in the previous session; don't you ever be afraid to do that, our memory can never be so frail as to forget who he is. Regarding the number of sessions, as well as the name of the patient and everything you need to know, you can keep everything easily recorded.

If a patient learns from me that I want him to improve his condition, if he can get to the point of having that desire himself because he assumes that his analyst is a doctor and, as a result, the doctor wants to cure him—on the other hand, he is there to be cured and he feels that the analyst wants to cure him—then the first step the patient will take will be to guess what the analyst considers to be the cure. This is another reason why the analyst must not feel desires that might be filtered in during the session; they might interfere not only with the analyst, but with the person being analysed—I am referring to conscious desires here. (Dr Bion is asked whether the wish to cure him might be present.) No kind of desire. Even the wish to understand is dubious. We must try to be like a sponge.

Allow me to draw your attention to this issue: the wish to cure and to be cured. Just wonder how you will be feeling tomorrow, the next and the following days, if you have a patient who feels you are a wonderful analyst, who says how gifted you are to heal people and that everything that happens is always for the better. The patient is afraid of the fact that if this continues much longer, he will hate the analyst and the analyst will hate him. It is terrible to be tied to someone towards whom we feel obligated to improve, to be always well, to be always cured. Besides, if the patient is always feeling that he must be cured and that everything is for the better, there is no chance for his difficulties in the analysis to become apparent, they will always be kept away. Then we will face this dilemma: analyst and patient get on really well, they like each other, and there is no risk of their growing apart, but there is an underlying fear that even though the relation is so perfect, even so, they might want to split up; how terrible will it be then if the patient lets the analyst know about his confusions, his bad issues, how will the analysis continue? If the analyst does not deal with these problems and the patient cannot bring them, then, there is no analysis. On the other hand, if the analyst analyses these problems and the patient allows it, both can feel that the analysis is really starting, but we must take into account that the patient's fear is, precisely, that then the analysis will come to an immediate end, because if there are long interruptions when everything is so perfect, what kind of interruptions will there be when it is just the opposite!

Question 3

Do you think we always can count on the adult part of the patient, in which a situation of mutual trust between patient and analyst is established?

Dr Bion: Indeed, we must do that. We can refer this to Freud's discovery of the fact that we must treat the patients when they are completely conscious, not when they are under hypnosis. The conversation is held with a conscious patient and the point is for that conscious patient to, somehow, communicate the novelties to the unconscious.

Question 4

How is the analytical contract established?

Dr Bion: The patient usually speaks with sufficient clarity about quite a lot of material and you can rely on several theories, but, basically, you feel if you want to work with the patient or if you don't. There is no substitute for feelings, you feel you are quite capable of working with most people, and with time only those patients who want to be helped will come to you.

I want to tell you to forget all those things we have been repeating here, because the more you have heard of the discussion we have held here, the less afraid I am of you being able to forget it. We don't know what will be happening in your next session, with this patient or with any of the others you are seeing, but the important thing is that when it happens we will know it is happening. We may not know what the interpretation is, but something is certain, if we do not know what is happening when it is happening, we cannot interpret it, no matter how good we are. This is what I mean when I use the concept of the model that lies between the patient and the interpretation, from a theoretical perspective.

INDEX